RENEWING YOUR HOPE

*My Daughter's Battle with
Cancer and Experiencing Many
Disappointments to Find Hope*

Tonia Wilkes

WESTBOW
P R E S S®
A DIVISION OF THOMAS NELSON
& ZONDERVAN

Scripture taken from the King James Version of the Bible.

WestBow Press books may be ordered through booksellers or by contacting:

WestBow Press
A Division of Thomas Nelson & Zondervan
1663 Liberty Drive
Bloomington, IN 47403
www.westbowpress.com
1 (866) 928-1240

ISBN: 978-1-5127-3730-1 (sc)
ISBN: 978-1-5127-3731-8 (hc)
ISBN: 978-1-5127-3729-5 (e)

Library of Congress Control Number: 2016905598

Print information available on the last page.

WestBow Press rev. date: 4/20/2016

CONTENTS

I dedicate this book to Randy, Kahlie, and Kason.
Sharing our story has become healing to our souls.

FOREWORD

Being the brother of Kahlie Blair Wilkes is an absolute privilege. I have a lot of memories of her despite being only six years of age when she died. There's still a big hole in my heart, but God is placing himself in that hole to completely fill the void.

This book is going to show you how it is possible to go through the worst trauma a human can emotionally experience and still be able to live the rest of your life with the peace of God. Being chosen by God is certainly a good thing! You know you're chosen by God when the most unpredictable circumstances come your way, and nothing ever seems to work out for you. This is why it's not something to boast about. It's not that God is against you; it's because that is the only way we will ever be able to fulfill the very plan he has for us. He doesn't want us to live the rest of our lives worried about the next chaotic event or in depression from the last one.

My mother, Tonia, is a living example of how your hope can be renewed after having all hope lost in complete darkness. My sister, Kahlie, is not dead. I believe she is with God right now. A person truly dies in this world when he or she is completely forgotten. Her life was a success, even though she didn't live long enough to graduate from college, have a family of her own, or find a cure for cancer. Her life is a success because she didn't benefit herself but the lives of others. It certainly hurts me that I can't say hello to her anymore, but God has shown me that everything is okay because she is with him.

You're probably going to read this Scripture a hundred times during this book, but every time something bad comes our way, I always remind myself of Romans 8:28: "For we know that all things work together for the good to those who love God, and are the called according to his purpose." This means bad times are coming for all of us, but we must have faith that God is doing it for the good. Serving God doesn't deliver us from having problems but makes our problems much easier to live with. If you know what true pain is, this book is just for you.

Remember, anyone must be able to understand true pain before truce peace can be understood. May our life's testimony be a blessing to you and encourage you to keep moving forward in your walk in the one true God.

Kason Wilkes

Preface

This is a mother's story of a family that loves God and believes he can do anything but fail and how they reacted when God didn't have the same plan they prayed for. It's a heartbreaking journey of how they had to give their daughter Kahlie back to God when she died of cancer at the age of thirteen. It's a story of hope and disappointments, but at the end, they still had hope. Renewing Your Hope Ministries believes that no matter what you are going through, God can renew your hope every day!

ACKNOWLEDGMENTS

To God be the glory for the things he has done in my life. I am in my sound mind because of him. He is my refuge and strength, and I could do nothing without him. I am thankful for my husband, Randy. He is my number one fan. He has always encouraged me to write my story even when I felt no one would want to read it. I thank my son, Kason, for believing in me and being the double portion in my life. He brings me so much joy. I am glad to see the calling of God work in his life. I am so thankful that God put my daughter, Kahlie, in my life to learn from her for thirteen years. She taught me more than anyone could ever know. I will tell her story until I die. I would like to thank my mom and dad for their love, support, and prayers for me when I knew at times they were worried about me. I am thankful that my family was in the room with me the morning Kahlie took her last breath. I thank God for Renewing Your Hope Ministries for being my saving grace. God has used this ministry to keep me and my family serving God with all of our hearts, souls, minds, and strength. Thanks to all of my family and friends who stood by me and helped me believe that I could do it.

CHAPTER 1

Kahliebug

On January 23, 1990, Kahlie Blair Wilkes, our beautiful baby girl, arrived and would change us and make a big impact in our lives forever. Our new little family was a dream of mine; I always prayed to be a wife and mother one day. God was blessing us far beyond what we could expect. Being a new mother was a scary thing. Can I take care of this beautiful gift from God? I'm responsible for her life and everything that goes with it. Am I doing everything right? I was nervous, but it became natural for me. I couldn't imagine loving anything more than this baby of mine. When we become parents, we get a tiny view of the love that God has for us. The only thing is, God loves us more.

When Kahlie was a baby, her nana gave her the nickname Kahliebug. Everyone loved it. We went to a fall festival and bought her a bracelet that had her name on it with a ladybug. Our family loves ladybugs, and they are a big part of our lives. (I'll tell you more about our family's special relationship with ladybugs later.) I loved all of the things Kahlie said and did as a toddler. We laughed and had so much fun together. We lived next door to Randy's grandmother, whom we called Maw. Kahlie loved her very much. Some mornings she would say, "Let's go eat breakthest with Maw." One day Kahlie wanted some chocolate cake, and she said, "Daddy, give me some chocolate clake." I can remember us laughing at how she mispronounced the words "cake" and "breakfast." We will hold on to those memories forever.

Kahlie was healthy and full of energy and laughter. She was singing at a very young age, and she lit up the room with her presence. I stopped working to be a stay-at-home mom to be with her every day. That was priceless to me. With me not working, though, money was tight. One day we went to my parents' house (Kahlie's nana and papa). Nana told Kahlie to take the whole box of cereal home with her. When we got into the car, I told Kahlie that I would have to scrape up some money to get some milk at the store. Kahlie said, "Momma, can we put some milk on layaway?" She always had a quick wit about her, even as a small child. She was a very active child who loved gymnastics and tae kwon do. From a very young age, she had a love for music and singing. She began to play the piano at the age of six and started playing the trumpet at the age of eight. She was very talented and played with her whole heart with great anointing. She loved being in the church band. She loved God and going to church. She was filled with the Holy Ghost at a very young age. She had a real experience of her own with God. She was going to need his power inside her for the rest of her journey.

I was so content with Kahlie that year after year went by with no thought of having another child. I had a dream one night that I was in the labor and delivery room having a baby, and the doctor said, "It's a boy." He handed my baby to me and said, "Kason." I woke up from my dream saying, "Kason." I believe God was telling me to have another baby. At that time, Kahlie was six years old. We felt like it was time for her to have a sister or brother but knew in our hearts from the dream that it would be a boy named Kason. I got pregnant soon after and was so excited. Six weeks into my pregnancy, I started spotting. I went to the doctor right away. I was having a miscarriage. We were so disappointed. But I knew what God had promised us.

I recovered from the miscarriage, and a few months later, I found out I was pregnant again. On September 18, 1996, Kason Blake Wilkes came into our lives and completed our family. Kahlie was so excited to have a baby brother. She proudly wore a shirt that her nana bought her that said, "I'm the big sister." Kahlie was a big helper to me. She was like a little momma to Kason. He was a live baby doll.

Our new family adventure began. It was just the three of us for six years, so it was like starting all over again with another child. God told me that Kason was my double portion. I didn't understand it at the time, but I knew that he would reveal it to me later. He was such a good baby with a gentle spirit and fit along with us just fine. Kahlie had a playmate, and we had lots of love and laughter in our home.

God sometimes whispers to us. During the summer of 1997, we were at the pool, and Kahlie jumped into the shallow end.

She had grown since the summer before, so she misjudged her jump, and it knocked the breath out of her. She couldn't catch her breath, so we called 911. As we were on the phone, Kahlie was able to get her breath back. We told the 911 operator that she was going to be okay, so we canceled the ambulance. Kahlie had never had health problems or an emergency before, and it shook us all up.

Kahlie loved to dress up. One day she came into the living room with a scarf wrapped around her head. Just for a moment, I thought of a cancer patient without hair, and it kind of startled me. I never mentioned any of that to her. Soon after, I was watching a movie about a woman diagnosed with leukemia, and I cried and cried. The movie was so touching that I watched it again.

Right at that time Kahlie began showing small signs of getting sick. We took her to the doctor. We first thought that the jolt and trauma from Kahlie jumping into the pool may have had something to do with her being sick, because that was when she began to have headaches. Your mind goes all over the place when you are looking for answers. The doctor said Kahlie had a viral infection and to bring her back if she didn't get any better.

A family from out of town came to visit our church. Their daughter started to run fevers and then became unable to walk. They brought her up for prayer, and Randy began to travail in the Spirit with intercessory prayer. He felt such a burden for her and the family. I feel like those were small whispers leading us to Kahlie's diagnosis. We are not always ready to hear God when he whispers, but his sheep know his voice. I didn't really understand those whispers until later.

CHAPTER 2

The American Dream

L iving the American dream may mean different things for different people. We owned our home and had two healthy children, a girl and a boy. We had a car, truck, boat, and two dogs. Randy worked at the fire department and had a landscaping business on the side so that I could be a stay-at-home mom. We loved God, and we were happy—not rich but happy. Our days consisted of homeschooling, play dates at the park, cooking all day, cleaning the house, and going to church. In the summer we lived at the pool.

In the summer of 1997, the American dream began to crumble. We were at the pool, and Kahlie told me she was ready to go home. You have to understand that my seven-year-old was never ready to leave the pool. I'd say, "Let's go home," and she'd say, "Let me dive off the diving board one more time, Momma." It was like pulling teeth to get my kids ready to go home. Now she was getting tired and took naps. That was something else she never did before. She lost her appetite, even for her favorite foods. We were all getting tan at the pool, but Kahlie would be pale. She was getting dark circles under her eyes, had headaches, and bruised easily. She became sicker every day. She ran low-grade fevers. When we took her to see the doctor the first time, they told us it was a viral infection. I had this mother's instinct that something wasn't right. A couple of days later, I took her back to the doctor. They ran more blood tests and sent us home. They told us that they would call us to let us know the results. I was a nervous wreck, waiting on the call. Kahlie hadn't wanted to eat anything all day. When we left the doctor's office, she wanted something to eat then.

When the doctor called, she said Kahlie's blood work came back with some concerns, and they were referring us to an oncologist. They gave me an appointment within the hour. The doctor asked if I could have someone come with me. My heart was beating so fast. I had a baby and a sick child, plus I was trying to make the dreaded call to Randy at work to come with me. I also called my mom to meet us there. I've never been around anyone who was sick before, so I didn't have any reason to know that an oncologist is a blood specialist cancer doctor. I seemed to hold it all together only because Kahlie was watching me and the expression on my face when I got off the phone. She was very smart and couldn't be fooled. I was dying on the inside with a tempestuous ocean raging inside me. I was nervous and felt like I was moving in slow motion, but everything felt like it was coming at me very fast.

We met the pediatric oncologist, Dr. Dannawi. He explained everything they would have to do to find out what was really wrong with our baby girl. I got lost in all the medical terminology and couldn't really focus. The doctor said they would have to do a bone marrow aspiration to get the diagnosis. Putting a big needle in my daughter's bone and spine was a hard thing for us to hear. He wanted to do it right then, but they would have to put Kahlie to sleep and she eaten not long before. We made an appointment to do it first thing the next morning. The doctor said to call him if her fever spiked.

We decided to take Kahlie to the mall so that she could buy a Barbie at the toy store. We were trying to do everything we could to make her happy. It was summer in Georgia and over 100 degrees that day. She was running a fever and had chills, so she wanted to wear her Barbie sweatshirt to the mall. We couldn't get out of there fast enough for Kahlie. She wanted to go home. We got into the car, and she said the heat felt so good to her. I checked her fever at home, and it was going up fast. I called the doctor, and he wanted to admit her into the children's hospital right away.

We checked into the hospital, and what a long and miserable night it was. I pleaded and fought with God. No, no! My baby girl was really sick with something bad, and I prayed and cried all night. Word got out pretty quickly about Kahlie, and family and friends began to show up at the hospital.

The next day she had a bone marrow aspiration. We had never experienced anything like it. I had never been sick and was only in the hospital when I had my children. Kahlie had never been sick. This was all new for us. They let Randy and me in the room, and the procedure was hard to watch. They put her in twilight mode sleep while they did it. When it was over, all she could do was cry because she was seeing double because of the medicine, and that scared her. Then the waiting began. This was going to be the beginning of many times we would have to wait on test results.

The doctor called us into another room with some nurses and other people I didn't know. It was a very scary thing. The doctor told us Kahlie had acute lymphocytic leukemia, cancer of the bone marrow and the blood. I don't think I heard another thing. It all sounded a blur. I was trying to process what leukemia was and how she got it. All I could see was my American dream, crumbling on top of me, and I couldn't breathe. I began to cry and hyperventilate. The only thing that I asked was, "Is she going to die? I wanted to get to Kahlie right away, wrap my arms around her, and love on her. I couldn't imagine my world without her. Randy was shaken up from all of the news, too. All we could do was cry. My momma stayed in the room with Kahlie while we got the results. She said that she could hear me crying all the way down the hallway. She was praying for us. She knew that the news couldn't be good from the sound of the cries. I'm sure she had to hide her pain from Kahlie.

They told us there was a 78 percent survival rate for her disease. They would have to start treatment right away. I went to Kahlie as soon as I could, held her in my arms, and loved on her like I had wanted to. I prayed for wisdom in what I would tell Kahlie about her disease. She had a glitter tube toy with stars inside. I told her the glitter was like her blood cells, and the stars were bad blood cells. The doctor would have to give her medicine to take the bad stars away from her blood. She wasn't devastated like I thought she would be. She was seven and didn't know what she was going to really have to face. Nor did we.

We were shocked with the news of cancer, but it seemed treatable. They told us about all the kids who survived leukemia and now lived a healthy life. We were hopeful and had faith that Kahlie would come through this. But there was always a fear that she would be among the small percentage who wouldn't respond to the treatment.

Kahlie went into remission within two weeks after starting chemotherapy. When Dr. Dannawi told us that she was in remission, it was a big sigh of relief. We were all happy that she was responding well to the treatment. Even though she went into remission, there was a three-year chemotherapy protocol. For the next three years, our whole life was going to revolve around the hospital. It would be worth it to keep our girl alive. You go to the ends of the earth to save your child.

Kahlie began to lose her blond hair not long after starting chemotherapy. It was devastating to a seven-year-old. I knew that it was just hair and would grow back, but when it is your own identity and self-esteem on the line, you tend to take it the hardest. It made us all see the true beauty inside Kahlie and her fight to survive. Her beautiful blue eyes shone so bright without hair.

The staff at the hospital told us they were going to make contact with the Make-a-Wish Foundation to grant Kahlie a wish. With Kahlie in remission, it was hard to believe she had a life-threatening disease. My seven-year-old wanted to go to Disney

World, of course. It was five months into the treatment, and she had it all planned out. Make-a-Wish flew us from the Atlanta, Georgia, to Orlando, Florida. They had a rental vehicle waiting for us at the airport to take us to Give Kids the World Village. It's a seventy-four-acre, nonprofit, "storybook" resort located near central Florida's most beloved attractions. There, children with life-threatening illnesses and their families are treated to weeklong, free, fantasy vacations. Sounds fun, huh?

The day before the trip I got a stomach virus and had to pack all day for a full-week trip. I woke up the next morning feeling better but not my best. We had just gotten on the airplane when Randy started feeling it come on him. He made it to Florida, and then it was bad. He had it a lot worse than I had. I was at the airport with a one-year-old, a seven-year-old, and a sick husband. I had to carry all of the luggage because Randy was too sick to help me. He lost the whole first day at the resort in the room while the kids and I enjoyed the pool and all of the attractions and entertainment in the village. We feared that Kahlie would be the one sick on the trip, but she felt great!

The first full day we went to Magic Kingdom. Randy felt somewhat better, but he didn't want a steak dinner. (He never turns down a steak dinner.) The days were filled with treating Kahlie like the princess that she was. We were first in line for everything and had backstage passes for after the shows. She loved meeting all the Disney characters. They gave her lots of personalized gifts. There were many perks on the trip that Make-a-Wish gave us. We were very thankful for the donations that people made to the foundation. It means a lot to the family to go on an all-exclusive trip when families are dealing with so much stress just trying to keep their children alive. The dream vacation of going to Disney World would have been us going at our own leisure, not battling cancer. Life doesn't always give you the best to work with, so we had to learn how to make the best out of every situation.

Getting back from Disney World and back to reality was not that easy to do. The new routines and schedules controlled our whole lives. While other kids were going to school and playing, I knew that Kahlie's childhood was going to be robbed. I had to fight not to get mad about that. I had to remember that God was in control of my American dream.

CHAPTER 3

Our New Normal

There's no need to go into deep detail about chemotherapy because we all know how sick it can make people. Kahlie had outpatient chemo throughout the week. Every three weeks she was admitted into the hospital for almost a whole week of chemo. Everything revolved around getting Kahlie well. It was our new normal. Kason was ten months old when she was diagnosed. I was so afraid that I would miss all of the first things he would do because of being at the hospital. We were always together. Kason was raised at the hospital with us. The only time he was not with us was when Kahlie had a procedure.

One day after a procedure, we went to get Kason from my pastor and his wife's house. We were in the living room, talking, and Kason started walking to me. Those were his first steps. I cried because I didn't want to miss anything. He had been on the verge of taking steps before we were admitted to the hospital. Raising a baby in the hospital was not my idea of how I wanted Kason to be raised. I knew that whatever we were going through, we would go through it together. We kept him entertained as much as possible. When this is your normal life, it doesn't feel strange to raise your child with a hospital full of doctors, nurses, and the wonderful staff who was a big part of making our experience a little more comfortable. Plus, all of them loved Kason.

During the first phase of treatment, for three years, Kahlie had to be on prednisone. We were told that she had to take this to protect her organs from the swelling caused by chemo. It protected her organs but made her outside swell. This was the monster medicine we all hated. The glorious, puffy prednisone face and body was a very hard thing for her to handle. She was a beautiful seven-year-old who had been very energetic and active, with a vibrant personality. Now she had weight gain, back pain, depression, anxiousness, heartburn, and the dreaded one … hunger!

I had to talk with Kahlie about body image because she was on prednisone, and the weight started coming on. She didn't like what it was doing to her body; she felt miserable, fat, and ugly. One day she didn't even want to go to the park to play with her brother because she didn't want to be seen that way. I told her that she was beautiful, and she needed that medicine to get well. She didn't want to hear it. She just wanted it all to go away. Her self-esteem took a big hit with no hair, weight gain, and big, round cheeks. Throughout the treatment we had to constantly reassure her of how beautiful she was. As she grew and got older, the weight balanced out, and of course her hair grew back. That made her feel somewhat better.

We fed her around the clock. Sometimes we would go out to eat and have to feed her before we left the house. She couldn't wait for the drive to get there and wait for us to order our food. There were times we stopped to get her something to eat on the way, and she ate it while we ordered our food. Plus, she was always the first one to order at the restaurant. We always ordered extra so that she would have plenty to take home. It was nothing to be up at 3:00 a.m., heating up spaghetti or anything left over from dinner.

All the food consumption caused other problems, like severe heartburn, acid reflux, and going to the bathroom a lot. She would be so miserable. You may think that eating all day would be so much fun, but it was awful for her. There were times the chemo made her have really bad sores in her mouth, and it was very painful for her. The acid reflux was unbearable. I can remember her asking me why God wasn't touching her. That was a very hard question for me to answer. I would cry because I didn't understand the answer myself. I told her that this was going to be our testimony. We still love God even though we may never know the answer.

She would cry and be moody and lethargic. The medicine made her back hurt so much. I had to pop her back regularly. She took the prednisone one week out of every month for three years. It took about two weeks after each dose before she was back to herself again, but the dreaded fourth week she started prednisone all over again. We planned our lives around the week she was off of that medicine, like when we went to Disney World. During all our trips, parties, and shopping, she felt free! We did, too, because she laughed and smiled again. We learned how to live with a trash can in the vehicle because of nausea. I'd never seen anyone throw up as much as my own daughter. It wasn't pleasant, and I hated seeing her that way. But there was nothing I could do. I felt helpless

On Kahlie's eighth birthday, we wanted to do some something very special for her, so we had a big party. I went all out and rented ponies and a clown. We had the whole park to ourselves. It was in January, so it was very cold outside. I made a big pot of hot chili for all of us to eat to try to stay warm. Lots of people showed up to celebrate Kahlie. The only problem was that her birthday landed on prednisone week. I almost didn't want to give her a party, but I knew that she'd be disappointed. She tried to have fun, but no matter how much we tried, she was miserable and didn't feel her best. I look back at her pictures of that party and see how everybody else had more fun than she did at her own party.

We prayed thousands of prayers, but the sickness didn't leave. We quoted thousands of Scriptures. We spoke positive words of healing, and nothing happened. That is the very moment your faith gets tested. Are we going to be mad at this invisible God who is silent in our trouble? Are we going to harden our hearts in the day of provocation (something that incites, instigates, angers, or irritates)? The Lord tells us in the Bible not to harden our hearts when we are in trouble. It was a choice to keep believing that God was for us and had a plan for all of us—regardless of how it looked.

It is easy to get frustrated at God. The children of Israel got so mad at God when times of hardship came along. He is God and wants people to have full trust and confidence in him in every situation of life. When we harden our hearts, the Lord said that we can't enter into his rest. I need rest and peace when I go through hard times. I don't want to live in doubt, confusion, anger, and frustration. I tried it, and I didn't like it at all. Our new normal was to trust God not only when he was showing his favor toward us but also when he seemed to be a million miles away.

It was a normal day at the hospital. Kahlie was having a routine bone marrow aspiration and spinal tap. I was having PMS issues, and my momma reached into her purse to give me something for pain. She told me to take one now and then one later that day. I was so focused on Kahlie's procedure and my pain that I didn't hear her say only take one. I popped both pills in my mouth. About ten minutes later, I was talking to a nurse and began to feel strange. The more I talked, the more I realized Momma had given me more than just a Tylenol. I had to dismiss myself and went straight to my momma, grabbed her, and asked, "What did you give me because I am high as a kite?" She frantically went to get her purse and found she'd grabbed the wrong bottle and given me strong pain medication. The week before she'd had surgery, so that is why she had pain medicine in her purse. She told me she didn't have her glasses on and couldn't see what she was doing.

The procedure room was all prepped and ready for us to go in. All the doctors and nurses were ready, but I wasn't because all I could do was giggle. I could barely stand on my own. I had to lean on Randy and the wall the whole time. While Kahlie was the one being sedated and put to sleep, I was in bad shape myself. All I could do was smile and giggle. Everyone asked me if I was okay. That was not something that I would normally do while Kahlie was having a serious procedure. After it was over, Kahlie slept awhile, and I went to let the medicine wear off from me, too. I'd never taken pain medicine like that before.

At lunchtime, Randy and I went across the street to get something to eat, and Momma said she would stay with Kahlie. We were going to bring her lunch back to her. As I walked over to the restaurant, I knew that the medicine hadn't fully worn off yet. As we were going back to the hospital, I stepped off the curb, missed my step, fell on my knees, and rolled over on my back. I had a big audience because it was the busiest time of the day, and we were at an intersection. I had a skirt on, and you could see the blood running down my legs. I skinned both knees but didn't feel a thing! I dropped Mom's lunch, and it was all mixed up in the to-go container. When we got back, the nurses were smirking because my momma told them what she had accidentally done to me. Kahlie's nurse had to clean me up and put bandages on my knees. Everyone knew something was wrong with me because I was acting way out of character. We always had to look for something to laugh about when we felt that life was way too serious and hard on us. It didn't feel normal, but it was going to be our new normal.

CHAPTER 4

The Lord Speaks

Being a stay-at-home mom was awesome, but many years into it, I began to put on a little weight. That was about the time I got pregnant with Kason. I didn't gain but twenty pounds with my ten-pound baby boy. I lost the weight after I delivered, but I still weighed more than I did before I had Kahlie. Kason was ten months old when Kahlie got sick. We began to have a crazy schedule with hospital visits for days, weeks, months and outpatient chemo. So we ate when and where we could. Over a six-month period, I gained more weight. I felt out of control. I was stressed and depressed and wasn't even thinking about poisoning my body. Randy had also put on some weight. I prayed and felt that the Lord spoke to me to take care of myself, eat healthfully, and exercise. Even amid chaos, he was going to give me the temperament and ability to do it the healthy way.

I made up my mind to be in the best health that I could be within my power to do so. I began to make better food choices and worked out seven days a week. I was very determined. I would work it in no matter what. I waited until Kahlie went to sleep at night before I left her to walk down the hallways of the hospital. When I was home, I did weights and walked. I made no excuses. I started studying nutrition and cooked very healthy meals when we were at home. Before I knew it, I'd lost sixty-two pounds without trying to diet. Whew! What a load off of me. I needed to be in great shape for everything I was going to face. I know what real struggles are. I know how easily you can forget about yourself, let yourself go, and give into temptations and convenience foods because life is so hectic. Jesus was my temperance and the desire I needed to be well in spirit, soul, and body.

That was in 1997, and by God's grace, I am still eating healthfully and working out. My family enjoys working out and eating well, too. Kason was five years old when we signed him up for tae kwon do. He did it for eight years. He is a third-degree black belt and was an instructor. We signed him up because we wanted him to have something on his own other than living a life in the hospital. We wanted to keep him active and get his mind off his sissy being sick. She was so proud of him. We would go to tournaments, and Kason would win first place. Kahlie would holler out, "Whew, that's my brother!"

We still work out together as a family on a regular basis. It would have been easy to lean on food because as Christians we know that alcohol and drugs are bad for our bodies. But food is also a drug. We tend to rely on that quick feel-good feeling, but in the meantime, it kills us when we eat bad food. God wants us to cast our cares on him, not to take our stresses upon ourselves.

Food can have a stronghold on many people. We fight in many spiritual battles, but food shouldn't be one of them.

I shared my story because I am a real woman who has had to deal with many issues with food and my body. We are under so much pressure, juggling a household and life's problems that come our way. On top of that, we're supposed to look good while doing it. Randy called me "wonder woman" one time. He thought he was giving me a compliment, but I told him I didn't want to be a wonder woman. I was doing it all and beginning to feel resentful doing it. It was a heavy load for me to carry, making sure everything got done. I was packing constantly for doctors' appointments and hospital trips. I was homeschooling, doing laundry, and cleaning my house when I was barely even there. I was cooking healthy meals, working out, and taking care of a toddler and a sick child. Oh, and don't forget I also had a high-maintenance husband. I had to break down and tell Randy that I could do it all, but I shouldn't have to do it all. I didn't need a first-place trophy; I just needed my sanity and some help. Randy stepped up and helped me a lot. I wouldn't have wanted to do it without him.

I stayed with Kahlie every night at the hospital. When Randy was off from work, there were times that he wanted to stay, but most of the time he stayed with Kason. He was a firefighter and worked twenty-four-hour shifts, so he dropped Kason off to me every morning that he had to work. My mom wanted to stay some with Kahlie so I could get out of the hospital and be with my husband and son. We were always on standby because we never knew what was going to happen. I look back now and can hardly believe what all we had to do. God gave us peace and strength in our chaos. I thank God for speaking to me about my health. I wouldn't have wanted to feel sluggish, tired, and drained while juggling life. God gave me the power. I could do all things through Christ because he was my strength.

Our exciting family trips were always fun. We made the time to take them. We liked to let our children experience all that we could afford to do. We live one hour and twenty minutes from Six Flags over Georgia, so we went every year. One year we wanted to go back the same week we did the year before. We all were excited to go. When we arrived, the parking lot was empty. Randy said, "We are the first ones here!" As we kept driving we noticed the closed sign on all of the parking ticket windows. Oh no! We felt like *National Lampoon's Vacation*. Do you remember the movie? The Griswolds drove cross-country from Illinois to California to go to Walley World, an amusement park, and it was closed for remodeling. We laughed so much all the way home. We kind of felt bad for the kids, so we bought them a trampoline that day. We later went back to Six Flags, but I checked to see if they were open before we went.

Before Kahlie got sick, Randy had been running from the calling to preach. At the age of sixteen, he felt a calling on his life. He served God but seemed to struggle with the full surrender of his calling. At times, he even struggled going to church. Kahlie's cancer was devastating to all of us. We all had to go to God in prayer and seek him. Randy sought God and cried out to him. When my heart is overwhelmed, lead me to the Rock that is higher than I. When life happens, we tend to confess our sins and bargain with God. Like, "God, if you heal Kahlie, I will do whatever you want me to do." He always knows the intent of our hearts. We can't fool God. Randy told the Lord that he would preach and do what God had called him to do.

As Kahlie began to go through treatment and seemed to be doing better and in remission, Randy slipped back into not wanting to preach or go to church as much anymore. All I could do as his wife was to pray for him and not nag at him. I sometimes took the kids to church by myself. He began to take up many hobbies to keep his mind off having a sick child and running from the ministry. His hobbies were football, tae kwon do, and Brazilian jujitsu.

This book would not be complete telling you the Jet Dry story. Randy was gone all day, trying out for an adult football league. I was home all day with the kids, cleaning the house and constantly picking up toys. Then the kids and I went to the grocery store. As I unloaded the car, Randy got home and asked the most horrible question ever: "What's for dinner?" I told him the long list of things I'd done all day and told him to fix himself a sandwich. He didn't like the fact that he didn't have a piping hot meal ready to eat as soon as he got home. He started complaining about the sandwich. I was under a lot of stress. Women, I don't recommend doing this, but I grabbed the bottle of Jet Dry and opened it. I squirted it onto his sandwich as he turned to the refrigerator to put up the mustard. I wasn't trying to kill him; I promise. But I also knew that he would taste the Jet Dry and spit it out. I watched as he took a big bite out of his sandwich. I could hardly keep my composure. Then he spit it out just like I thought he would. He asked me if the turkey meat was bad. I told him no, I had just bought it. He was so mad that he left the house to grab something out. It took me a couple of days to finally tell him what I'd done. That was a long time ago, and we laugh about it now. Don't judge me. I'm a changed woman, and Randy is a changed man. I now give bottles of Jet Dry to all of the women in our church who get married as a joke for their husbands.

I always prayed and fasted for my husband when he wasn't coming to church. I put prayer cloths under his side of the mattress. I never gave up hope that he would be back to church and fully surrender his life to the calling that God had on him. I was at church testifying one service and felt a boldness of God come over me to say that by the end of the year, Randy would be back in church, say yes to the calling, and never leave again. I was anointed and felt God's presence while saying it. It felt great! When I sat down I thought that I was an idiot. What did I just say? Was it excitement and expectation, or was it truly from God? I couldn't take it back; it was out there. I had never spoken anything so bold before. That was in the summer when nothing was happening. The more I prayed, the worse he got. He was so miserable. December came, and it didn't look good at all. I got up in church and said that even if God didn't bring Randy back, I was still going to believe and pray for him. I was so afraid that it wasn't going to happen. I was afraid that I'd missed God and spoken on my own. I have to admit that my faith was shaky.

There were only two more services left before the end of the year. Our pastor was having a fiftieth birthday luau, and I invited Randy, not even thinking that he would come. I couldn't believe he wanted to go. We were having live entertainment for the party. Kahlie and I were asked to sing, and I picked one of Randy's favorite songs, "More than Wonderful," by Sandi Patty. The presence of the Lord was in that place. You have to imagine us at a luau, dressed in luau attire, with coconuts and pineapples all around for decoration. Randy began to feel the presence of God and wept. All the men prayed for Randy. It was a sight because they were all wearing straw hats. Randy threw his hands up into the air and totally surrendered to God. The women prayed, too, in our grass skirts and with flowers in our hair and Hawaiian leis around our necks. God rocked that party! That night, God showed me that anytime he wanted to, he could touch Randy's heart—even at a birthday luau.

The last service of the year was a watch night service, and Randy was baptized over again. He has never looked back. God has a sense of humor to move on Randy at the very end of the year. That was cutting it close. But when God's speaks, he is always on time. He spoke to me and said, "By the end of the year." I was going to need Randy to be strong in the Lord with me on our journey of life because we were going to face the highest mountain together. I am glad that I never stopped praying for Randy. I thank God for his saving grace every day.

Three years of chemo seemed to drag by. But when the time was near, I began to struggle with the thought of Kahlie not being under a doctor's care every week. The last day of chemo should have been an exciting day for us, but my emotions were mixed. A nurse gave us a book about not being in treatment anymore and what to expect with our emotions.

We went out to eat afterward to celebrate, but I cried the whole time. Kahlie thought they were happy tears. I never wanted her to know the real reason. I wanted to believe that everything was going to be great, but I also knew the reality of what could happen. In the three years we were at the hospital, we saw many children live and do well; we also saw some die. That was the reality we lived in.

It was a bittersweet day for us and the hospital staff. They were a big part of our life. We were now going to the hospital once a month for a checkup. When the cancer patients leave from their last chemo treatment, they never want to see them come back because of a relapse.

The Lord spoke to me and put it on my heart to give Kahlie a celebration for life party. She had endured a lot over the last three years and deserved a big celebration. We also wanted to thank all the doctors, nurses, and staff that had helped us over the last three years. No more chemo, needles, and don't forget prednisone. By this time, Kahlie was ten years old and full of opinions. She planned her party all by herself. She picked out the invitations and chose the food that she wanted. I took her shopping, and since she couldn't decide which dress she wanted, we bought her two. She wore one for the ceremony and one for the reception. My sister and I took her to get her hair done at a salon. She was so beautiful. A few friends helped me cook and cater for the big event. We had our church band come to play. Kahlie played her trumpet, sang, and played the piano. She wrote and gave her own speech. She was who we were celebrating, but we were giving God all the glory for the things he had done. Lots of family, friends, and hospital staff came to help celebrate. It was a great night! No more chemo was a happy occasion to celebrate, but Kahlie being alive was an even greater thing to celebrate. Don't wait until someone is old to celebrate his or her life because you never know if tomorrow will ever come. Celebrate every day!

After the treatment and party were over, we tried to adjust to not having such a busy schedule anymore. It felt so strange, but it was freeing. We took time to play hard, and we were enjoying Kahlie feeling great every day. She was able to do all the things she couldn't do while in treatment. Every day that she wasn't sick was such a big blessing to us. Kahlie was back to her real self again. Every month we went to the doctor for a checkup, and Kahlie would have a clean bill of health.

Many months went by, and I felt I could really exhale in relief. Then one day I was praying at home and the Lord spoke to me, telling me to put on my seat belt. I wasn't quite sure exactly what he meant. At first I thought that we had already been through the worst, so maybe he was going to take us up in some kind of spiritual graduation, reward us for what we had been through, or take us higher in him faster. I just thanked the Lord for speaking to me.

We were at church one service, and Randy was getting a great touch from God. It was one of those blessings that put him to the floor. When he got up, a church minister told Randy that the Lord spoke a word for him. He told him that "God is fixing to take you and your wife through something that only God can help you with, and no man will be able to help you." He told

Randy that with tears in his eyes. Okay, God was speaking to us now, but we still didn't know why.

That summer Kahlie started complaining about her foot. We just thought that she jammed it jumping around and playing hard with her brother. We went to Six Flags and walked all over the park. By the end of the day, Kahlie was crying because of her foot. Her daddy had to carry her to the car from the exit. We were very worried. We were coming up on her one-year anniversary of being chemo-free.

The next day we took her to see the doctor, and they ran the normal blood work they did every month for her checkup. Everyone said how great Kahlie looked. We told Dr. Dannawi about her foot, and, of course, he was concerned. We waited for the test results and then received the worst news ever. Kahlie had relapsed with cancer at the age of eleven. We were blown out of the water and so devastated. She was doing so well; how could this happen? Words cannot express the shock that came over our bodies. The foot pain she was experiencing was one of the symptoms of leukemia.

Sometimes you don't put together what the Lord says right away. Later on we began to remember what the Lord told me about putting on my seat belt. What happens when you have a major car accident and don't have a seat belt on? It could kill you. The Lord was telling me to put on my belt of truth—the Word of God. It was going to be the only thing that would save me and Randy from the horrible and devastating crash we were experiencing. What the minister told Randy was going to be very true. No person could help us for sure.

The worst thing I had to do was tell Kahlie that she relapsed and would have to start over with a more-aggressive treatment plan. The news got to the staff very quickly, and they all came to us. Kahlie was crying and asked me if she was going to die. I had to console her and tell her that we were trusting God for her to get better. I kept telling her I was sorry. I somehow felt like it was my fault as a mother. The doctor told us we had a very sick girl. That was so hard to hear because Kahlie looked the best she had in a long time. Cancer deceives.

I needed to hear from God. The Lord spoke this Scripture for me to stand on: "Not that we are sufficient of ourselves to think anything as of ourselves; but our sufficiency is of God" Second Corinthians 3:5. That went right along with the words, "No man will be able to help us." I could hardly breathe and couldn't comprehend why she had to relapse. I had so much pent-up hurt that I had to get out of the hospital for a while. I got into my car and screamed and beat the steering wheel over and over again until I had no voice left. At that moment I felt so much pain. I wished it had of been me fighting the cancer, not my daughter. The cancer had come back with a vengeance to take her life.

It's a helpless feeling to have no control over what God's will is for your life. God had the power to stop her from relapsing, but he didn't. It had to be God's perfect plan. His ways are always perfect. This life is a vapor, and God is now and the future, so no matter what you are facing, you have to give it to the One who controls everything—the almighty God. Nothing can happen to you that God doesn't allow. We know that all things work together for the good of them who love God, to those who are called according to his purpose. All we can see are the pain and discomfort. We look at things through our natural eyes. God wants us to look at things through his eyes. He promised us that he would work it for the good. We just have to trust him. God's ways are so much higher than our ways, and his thoughts are higher than our thoughts. Through this hard time in our lives, we chose to cling to his unchanging hand and trust that he knew what was best for our lives.

When I was young, my mom bought me a new Bible and wrote this inscription in it: "God is your refuge and strength and a very present help in time of trouble." As a young girl, I would never knew the full meaning of that Scripture. Now, as an adult who has gone through trouble in my own life, I'm glad to know that God has been my refuge and strength, and he has always been with me in my trouble. His words can only come alive to you if you listen when he speaks.

The treatment was so hard on her body that the chemo through the spine damaged the nerves, and she lost the ability to walk. The hits kept on coming. Now our eleven-year-old has cancer and is paralyzed. Now we had to learn how to take care of a paralyzed child physically and emotionally. We hoped that when she got better that she would walk again. They started her on physical and occupational therapy right away. They later sent us to a specialist to see if she would be able to walk again, and the test came back that she would not. The only reason we didn't completely melt down was because we still hoped and prayed for a full miracle one day. We always spoke to Kahlie with great hope that God was going to heal her.

It was a rough transition of living for us and especially for Kahlie. She went back into remission. Then we got the news Kahlie was in kidney failure, and we had to rush her to the pediatric intensive care unit. Thank God her full kidney functions came back, but right after that, she began to run very high fevers. The hits kept coming. Her immune system was down so low because of the chemo. The doctor ordered an MRI of her whole body. The results were almost unbelievable. The doctor told us Kahlie had a fungal infection. She had mold growing in her brain, kidneys, and spleen. The doctor told us there wasn't a cure. Our hearts sank. We couldn't believe that Kahlie was back in remission, but her body had been so broken down that though she may not die from leukemia, she would die from complications of treating the disease.

The bad news sent hot, tingling waves from my head to my toes, like hot oil running down my body. The sense of fear that came over me was overwhelming. Kahlie had to have a neurosurgeon go into her brain for a biopsy. The results came back that it was in all four layers of her brain. Kahlie should have been having seizures and been unable to speak. She never lost her ability to think clearly. That in itself was a miracle.

The doctor told us about a medicine that wasn't FDA approved but was in a study form. He asked us if we would like to try to get in on the study. He said there was nothing else they could do. We were so desperate that we prayed it would work. I remember signing the paper with shaky hands and thinking that I might be signing away my daughter's life.

It took a week for the medicine to start working. Her high fevers stopped. The doctors and nurses were amazed to see her overcome every obstacle. When Kahlie was the sickest with the brain fungal, there was a doctor who often came and checked on her. Kahlie had a great memory, and one day when she came to see her, Kahlie said, "Happy birthday." The doctor was so amazed that she remembered that it was her birthday. A few weeks later, Kahlie had another MRI, and the fungus was gone in her kidneys and spleen, and had shrunk in her brain. She was beginning to start feeling better.

When Kahlie had lost all her hair multiple times, her hairstylist gave her a wig. After she was finished with her treatment the first time, she had really long, beautiful, thick, curly hair. We took the wig to the hospital, and we all tried it on. We laughed until we cried. We were so loud that nurses and staff came into our room to see why we were laughing so hard. It was a great moment. My mom called while we were laughing and told us to enjoy every moment and memory that we could, and for me to call her back later. It was such a great moment I will never forget. I will keep it in my heart forever.

CHAPTER 5

Worship

When Kahlie relapsed, she was admitted into the hospital. Treatments would be a few days or a week at a time, but this time we were in the hospital for three months straight. It was beginning to wear on her and all the family. She was getting homesick, and so was I. She would cry and say, "Momma, I want to go home." She was getting very depressed and begged her doctor to let her go home for just a few hours. The doctor knew Kahlie was stable enough to leave for a short time, so he wrote her a two-hour pass.

Kahlie wanted to go home, and she wanted to go to church. It was a Sunday excursion. She was very weak and fragile, but she was very excited to get out of that hospital, even if only for two hours. The hospital staff ran around, trying to find her a wheelchair for us to take her out in. We had to order a special one for her but hadn't received it yet. We let our neighbors know what we were doing, and when we pulled into our yard, the neighbors were there to greet her. She was so happy. Her daddy carried her into our house, and she cried the whole time. He carried her through every room so that she could see it. She said that she missed being home. It was very emotional. We only had two hours and needed to make the best out them and make it count.

We went to church and wheeled her inside. She had no hair, no eyebrows, and no eyelashes because of the chemo. She was frail and had lost a lot of weight, but she didn't care. She was just glad to be there. The church band began to play a song: "I Am Blessed", by Joe Ford "I am blessed—I am blessed—every day that I live I am blessed. When I wake up in the morning til I lay my head to rest—I am blessed—I am blessed." I watched Kahlie sing that song with tears streaming down her face; she was worshipping in the spirit. That day forever changed the way I worshipped. How could a very sick child with all kinds of life-altering challenges sing praises to a God when it seemed that she had nothing good going for her. I realized then what she already knew. She had Jesus, and she was blessed. He is the giver of eternal life, and that was her hope. True worship is when you don't understand God's plan but you worship him anyway. Worship gets you through the hardest times in your life because it shifts your focus from your problem to the problem solver.

I was born to worship. I can remember as a child loving God and his presence. Through the years, I have learned what true worship is. It's not just lip service or bodily exercise. It comes from deep within and is all about God, not you. We are in love with God first, and we want to praise him because he first loved us. The purpose of our worship is to glorify, honor, praise, and exalt

God. True worship is a dying to your will. He wants us to give a sacrifice of praise when we don't feel like it or when we don't think God is for us at times. He wants us to worship him in spirit and in truth. Worship is not manipulation. We can't control God's plan just by worshipping him. Our praise is a constant reminder to us and him that we know God is in control. Jesus prayed in the garden, "If it be possible to let this cup pass from me." But ultimately he prayed, "Not my will but thine be done" Matthew 26:39.That should be all of our prayers. I would never discourage anyone from praying for complete healing or for something that you desire, but you should always have the mind-set to say, "Not my will but thine be done."

When I was young, a minister came to our church and said, "If you dance in the Holy Ghost, you will never have a nervous breakdown; it empowers you to be victorious." That has always stuck with me. I have always loved to dance before the Lord. It is liberating and freeing to my spirit. Plus, it's what the Lord asks us to do. David danced before the Lord with all his might. He was unashamed to worship his God.

I realize there are times in our lives when it's not the season to dance. It may be a season to mourn. But I promise that the season to dance will always be appointed: "To appoint unto them that mourn in Zion, to give unto them beauty for ashes, the oil of joy for mourning, the garment of praise for the spirit of heaviness; that they might be called trees of righteousness, the planting of the Lord, that he might be glorified" (Isaiah 61:3).

I have had to worship out of my deepest pain, but God's presence is always there to lift me and be my strength. We are blessed when we mourn because we recognize that Jesus is our comforter. Job stated in the Bible that "The Lord gave, and the Lord hath taken away; blessed be the name of the Lord" Job 1:21. The act of true worship is more than just getting the great result of what you have been praying for. You praise him when he gives and when he takes away. Sometimes when we pray we may not be able put our thoughts into words. The Spirit helps our infirmities. The Spirit intercedes for us with groaning that cannot be uttered. When we pray like this, he is really praying for us. The result will always be yes to his will.

If the Lord has ever taken you to the most holy place, you'll never be the same again. It's the deepest place of worship that you can go before you are out of this world and present with the Lord. Just like taking time for your spouse every day, you have to take the time for an intimate relationship with God. Entering into his presence every day has changed my life. He will draw near to you when you draw near to him. That is the awesome thing about seeking God. The more you seek him, the more you find him. We tend to allow life to interfere with our relationship with God. The cares of this world and the lust of many things choke out the Word and cause you to be unfruitful in your life. Worship is a choice. Don't let anything take away your praise!

We were riding in the van one day, going to lunch, and the song "Jesus, Lover of My Soul" was playing. We all began to sing, and Kahlie began to cry. When the song was over, Kahlie said, "My world has fallen, and I never want to let him go." She had a real relationship of worship with Jesus, and he was the lover of her soul. That is more than a mother can ever hope for.

We were riding home from chemo one day and she was writing her first song, "Give God the Glory." She sat at the piano when we got home and put the music to the lyrics all by herself. I was so amazed. At the time, she was only ten years old. She was in her third year of chemo treatments. I knew at that moment that she was very talented in the gift of music. God was doing a quick work in her life. As she went through many struggles, more songs would come. I encouraged her to worship him in her music and to let God use her. She was beginning to be such a blessing in our church and to others.

Kahlie, my friend, and I were worshipping in the living room with some music playing one night, and the presence of the Lord began to fall on us. Kason was in the bed with his daddy. He woke up and came into the living room. He sat on my lap and began to cry. I watched how God was touching both of my children. Kason was only five years old at the time; Kahlie was twelve. She began to pray for her brother, and he was filled with the Holy Ghost. Randy woke up and came in the room. He was so excited to see what God was doing in our children's lives. When God is the center of your home or your life, he can fill you anywhere and anytime. All God wants is our true worship.

CHAPTER 6

Kahlie Rejects Chemo

Kahlie had chemo, and it was a normal day. When we got home, she began to break out in a rash and started to itch. I gave her some medicine, and then she was fine. The next day, Kahlie complained that she was having a hard time catching her breath. We rushed her to the hospital. They gave her some medicine, and she was fine again. Our family was together on most trips to the hospital, but this time Randy was working. I had Kason with me while Kahlie was getting outpatient chemo. He was six years old at the time. This time when they gave her the chemo, she instantly was unable to breathe right before my eyes. She looked at me in desperation and fear, wanting me to help her, but I couldn't do anything but stay out of the way and watch the doctor and nurses do their jobs and pray. Kahlie began to turn blue, and they had to intubate and give her medicine. She was going into full anaphylactic shock. I tried to shield Kason from the trauma, but it was impossible. A nurse called Randy and my mom to tell them what was going on. Kahlie was taken to the pediatric intensive care unit. They told us that Kahlie was allergic to the chemotherapy; her body was rejecting the medicine. We couldn't believe it. What was going on? She was in remission; this couldn't be happening. The doctor told us the chemo she was taking was the very best, but she could never have it again or she would die. There was an alternative, but it wasn't as powerful and might not keep her in remission.

Everyone was on standby the first time they gave her the new chemo. They also gave her some medicine to help her just in case she started to go into anaphylaxis again. She did just fine. The next time Kahlie received the chemo, she started to itch a little but not very much. I was getting very nervous though. The next time she received the chemo she went into full anaphylactic shock again. We were desperate for God to heal her completely. We had hoped that this was what God was telling us. No one will be able to help you; only God will be able to. I prayed, "God, this is your opportunity to do what you do best. Show up and show out. We will tell the whole world of your goodness and your miracles." That was our prayer for Kahlie to stay in remission. She was already two years into her relapsed three-year chemo treatment. God was our only hope. The doctor told us Kahlie had no other options.

He told us to come once a week for blood work and checkups. It was a very fearful day, but I had it in my mind that she was going to be okay, free from that horrible chemotherapy. We had to tell Kahlie that her body needed a rest from the chemo because it was hurting her, and we would just go for checkups every week.

I didn't want to crush her spirit and tell her that she would never be able to finish her treatment, and there was a possibility that she could relapse from cancer. While we were going for her checkups every week we pointed out a growth on her leg that look like a tumor. What else? This emotional rollercoaster has got to stop! They tested it for cancer, and it wasn't, thank God. It had to do with complications of paralysis.

Kahlie was on the bed one day, lifted her leg up with her hands, and it snapped. We took her to the hospital, and she had broken her leg and needed surgery. We had a routine checkup for a bone marrow aspiration and spinal tap. This day was like any other visit. She had many of these procedures over the past six years. This was to make sure that Kahlie was still in full remission. It was always nerve-racking for us no matter how many times she had them. We waited on the doctor to come back and tell us that Kahlie was fine. But when he peeped his head into our hospital room, I knew that something wasn't right. Over the last six years we learned his mannerisms. He also asked us to step out of the room, which was different. He took us to another room to tell us that the leukemia was back; she had relapsed. He was shaken up himself and had tears in his eyes. He cared for Kahlie during the whole treatment. Kahlie loved him. My heart sank in disbelief. Was God's will being played out in front of our eyes? Was she going to die? I wanted to lean to the promise that God would help us, and Kahlie would be healed without chemotherapy. Yes, that has to be the end of the story. This was going to be accepting God's will, and I wasn't ready for that yet.

When we found out about her relapse, we knew that Kahlie broke her leg because of cancer in the bone marrow. Randy and I talked and prayed about it at length and decided not to ever tell Kahlie that she had relapsed. She would be devastated. How do you tell your thirteen-year-old that she is going to die? Kahlie was near death many times through the years, and she always came out victorious. Our only hope was for God to give her a complete healing. We were at the Red Sea with no other options but God. Not knowing God's plan for our lives, yet still trusting him no matter what.

I had to get to the place just like the three Hebrew boys. I said, "Whether she lives or dies, I will not bow." That is never an easy statement even when there is no one to bow to literally. When we lean to our way and not God's, we are bowing to an idol that is ourselves.

We left the hospital with the worst news anyone could ever receive. As the days went by, the nurses came to our house to visit us. Kahlie knew that she was very special to them. God surrounded us with the best medical team. They loved Kahlie and emotionally supported our family in every way. They knew our faith in God was strong. Some of the nurses said that when they entered our room, there was a peaceful presence. That was saying a lot because in my flesh, I was wrestling with feeling stressed out, negative depressing vibes, doubts, and fears. Our faith in Jesus as our Prince of Peace stood the test of time. It was all of him and none of me.

One time we were at home, having a few friends over to pray, sing, and worship. I was playing the piano, and Randy had an encounter with an angel passing through the hallway. He saw a large shadow of light. We were all encouraged. After everyone left, we were watching Animal Planet on TV. I glanced over to the hallway and thought I was seeing things. I also saw the angel in the form of a large shadow of light. It moved slowly from Kahlie's room through the hallway. I screamed out, "I saw the angel!"

The next day, Kahlie, Kason, and I were practicing music. Kason was on the drums, and in the middle of the song, Kason jumped off and ran to me. He looked like he'd seen a ghost. He said, "Momma, I saw the angel." I knew by the way he acted that he wasn't just copying us from last night. Kahlie was so disappointed that she hadn't seen the angel. Randy and I believe it was her angel. Something so supernatural was what we really needed to know that God was near.

We were just trying to make every moment count, not knowing when Kahlie was going to start getting sick. She felt good and looked great. We wanted to do anything she wanted to do. The hospital made arrangements for us to take another trip through another organization. Kahlie wanted to go shopping. She was thirteen years old and knew how much fun it was to shop. She wanted to go to the Mall of America in Bloomington, Minnesota. We flew there. The altitude was different from Georgia's. Kahlie's platelets (cells that circulate in the blood and clot to keep us from bleeding) were low, and that with the change in altitude caused her nose to bleed throughout the trip. Still, she ran us all over that mall. Randy and Kason were thrilled about the amusement park inside the mall, so we would shop, ride the rides, and eat. That made all of them very happy.

Kahlie loved shoes, so we went shopping in most of the shoe stores. She had a cut on her foot, and because her platelets were low, it began to bleed. I couldn't stop the bleeding, so I grabbed some paper out of the shoeboxes and pressed her foot to help it stop. Kahlie was worried that her daddy would get upset, so she said, "Momma, don't tell Daddy that I was bleeding. It will upset him." She always wanted to protect us, and we were always trying to protect her.

We watched Kahlie enjoy the trip during the day, but when we were back at the hotel at night, we would break down in the bathroom and cry. We knew that this would be the last family vacation for us if God didn't give us the miracle we so desperately needed.

Before we left for the trip, Kahlie's friends wanted to give her a big going-away party. They didn't know that it truly was a going away for Kahlie. I watched as her friends celebrated who she was, and they made her feel special and loved. What a great night!

CHAPTER 7

The Big Move

Anyone who knows Randy and me knows that we are not conventional and ordinary. When Randy wanted to start his own lawn service business, he made cards and flyers to pass out. We ran all over town, passing them out. But we didn't own any lawn equipment. We waited until we got calls and then bought the things we needed and upgraded as the business grew. When you have a person with a handicap and in a wheelchair, it is much harder when you don't have a handicap-accessible home. We did put in a wheelchair ramp to help some, but inside the house, Kahlie couldn't move around on her own. We prayed about moving. We wanted it to be God's will because we had lived in our home for ten years.

We were in a church service out of town, and a man visiting from Africa looked at us and said, "God wants you to sell your house." We were shocked because we had told no one what we'd been praying about. We called a realty company to help us sell.

We prayed that if it was God's will, we would sell within the six-month period of the contract. We were crazy to embark on this big adventure. We were very scared because we had a daughter dying from cancer if God didn't heal her. I was busy cleaning, painting, and preparing to have an open house ready any time of the day. We had a buyer really fast. There was just one problem … we didn't have anywhere to live. That day we ran around town to look at houses, and the second house we looked at was the one we wanted. It had been on the market less than a week. We packed up to get ready for the move right before our trip to Minnesota and the Mall of America for a week. I told you we weren't conventional. We got back late the night before the big move. I had accidently told the GA Power Company to disconnect the power on the wrong date, so when we got home, we were in the dark.

The day of the big move we rented a moving truck to make it easier on everyone. Family and friends showed up to help. We couldn't have done it without them. The move was bittersweet because if Kahlie did pass away, we were leaving our home and all the memories that went along with it.

The first night in our new home we all slept on mattresses off the floor of the living room. We were trying to hold on to every memory that we could. We had the video camera on Kahlie's face most of the time to catch every moment we could. She helped us paint and clean. We didn't need music because she would sing loud and crazy songs to entertain us. We laughed as we enjoyed her company every day. While Kahlie slept at night, I stayed up late to unpack and paint so we could spend time together during the day.

I put life off for her. I was running off adrenaline. I felt deep in my heart that I wasn't getting the house ready for Kahlie to live in ... I was getting it ready for a funeral.

Kahlie was so excited to decorate her room and bathroom. She had bought everything new at the Mall of America. We shopped until we dropped ... literally. Kahlie heard on the news that it was snowing a lot in North Carolina, and she wanted to go. So we packed up and drove six hours. My mom and my brother went with us. The kids loved the snow. There is not much that you can do in a wheelchair, but just being in the snow made her happy. On our drive back, we were going to stop and eat. Kahlie turned to me and told me that she didn't want to die. The whole van became silent. We all had tears in our eyes. We lost our appetites and drove home. I always wanted to encourage her that she was in God's hands and that she was going to be okay. I was dying inside. She could feel the change in her body, and she was starting not to feel well

We lived in the new house two months when it all began to change. It had been four months since Kahlie had relapsed. She took a turn for the worse. Her health began to decline, and she needed to be on oxygen all day. Home health brought medical equipment to our home. Kahlie began to lose her appetite and sleep a lot. She developed a bed sore from lying down. Right after she became paralyzed, she had a bad bed sore and had to have plastic surgery. Keeping her turned all day and night was a full-time job. She was getting too weak to do it herself. My momma started spending the night with us a lot to help us out. We took turns sleeping in the bed with her. When she was well, I made her work for my kisses. I'd make her rise up in the bed to reach me, which made her stronger. She loved that game. Her daddy often played silly games with her. He wrote her songs and made her laugh until she cried.

There was beginning to be a change in the atmosphere. The reality was closing in on us. We are not promised a tomorrow, so we should live each day as if were our last. Psalm 90:12 teaches us to number our days, so we may apply our hearts to wisdom.

Kahlie got sick with pneumonia because her immune system was so weak. We thought that it was the end. She fought through and got over it like she had with everything else. Kahlie was wise beyond her years. I told her that she was thirteen going on thirty. She had been a very sick girl off and on for over six years, but this time she somehow knew she was worse. Our home was an open house for all our family and friends to stop by to see Kahlie anytime. I am thankful for the love, support, and prayers that we received. A home is supposed to be a safe place, but I couldn't get settled in because I feared that we were going to live in that home without Kahlie. It was hard to be excited about the move and our new home. I would have traded it all and lived in my car to have her healed.

C H A P T E R 8

I Need Your Mercy

have said before that Kahlie was wise beyond her years. Mother Teresa once said, "I alone cannot change the world, but I can cast a stone across the waters to create many ripples." Kahlie was a young girl who had a ripple effect on many people. I will never know how many lives she touched on this earth. She knew that God had plans for her and to give her an expected end.

When Kahlie was twelve years old, she wrote a song, "I Need Your Mercy." While she was singing it to me for the first time, she had tears rolling down her cheeks. I knew that it came from God.

I Need Your Mercy

Sometimes in the dark I seem so scared,
But I know that you are there 'cause you are God.

I need your mercy; I need your grace.
I need your strength to get me through this.
When I feel you, it's a sweet peace within.
Lord, come and cleanse this heart in me.
I need your mercy

The cross seems so heavy I can't seem to bear.
The road is long; keep me in your
care, you are Lord of Lords

Copyright by Kahlie Wilkes

In the first verse, Kahlie wasn't talking about being scared of the literal dark. When you are in the dark, you are unaware of what you can see, or you are not in the know of what is going on. Kahlie was afraid of what was going on in her life, and she was scared. But ultimately, she knew that God was there with her. She knew that she needed God's mercy and grace to get through this trial a twelve-year-old should never have to face. The cross was heavy for her, and the road felt long because she started her hard journey at the very young age of seven. She never doubted that he was Lord of Lords. He was her ruler, and she knew that he was working this for the good even though we didn't understand. What a profound and powerful song for a twelve-year-old to write. She sang her song to many people, and now I carry it on to be a blessing to others. I felt the Lord told me that he would still use her whether she lived or died. That is why I had to write this book. It was like fire shut up in my bones. The timing was now! I have put it off long enough. I may not reach the world with her story, but maybe she will continue to have a ripple effect.

Kahlie missed out on a lot of things when she became paralyzed and bound to a wheelchair. She loved the snow so much. We always took her to see snow if it didn't snow in our town. Our hospital wanted to do something special for all the children and their families, so they rented a snow machine one December. They created a snow mound for the kids to slide. Kahlie was trying to be happy for Kason as he was having a great time sledding down the hill, but I could see the tears roll down her cheeks. We didn't stay there long because I knew that she wasn't able to sled, and she was disappointed. We knew that life was going to be very different for her.

Waiting is something that we became great at and not by choice. When you are dealing with hospital time you may show up at 7:30 a.m. for surgery, and they call you back five hours later. We sometimes had to wait until the next week for test results and spent the whole weekend waiting impatiently. One day while waiting, the Lord gave me a song.

Waiting on You

Something beautiful in my life is what he's making today.
I felt I've cried my last tear; Lord, I long to
feel you near while I'm waiting on you.

Let me keep loving you while you are loving me.
Let me know that I'm your child and that you care.

Until your work is done in me, remind me to see
Your love while I'm waiting on you.

His promises are true even if the skies not blue.
The rain will come, and it will go, but
There's one thing I know: his love he wants to show.

Copyright by Tonia Wilkes

Sometimes while waiting, we think that it's God's punishment, but it is truly God's love. No one likes to wait—or am I the only one? I had to pray that I could love him while he was showing hard love back to me. You see, waiting was renewing my strength, but I wanted it the quick and easy way. God knows how long it takes to work something beautiful in our lives. He is not holding any good things back from us; he just has his perfect timing. Kahlie always sang the second verse. No matter if the sun is shining or not, God's promises are true. Sometimes in life the rain or storms will come, but there's one thing I know; his love he wants to show. In every situation that comes—good or bad—we believers have to hope that God is showing his love and favor to us if we just only wait on it. The only way we can do that is with his mercy.

Throughout the times of her treatment we met some awesome families. We saw children die from cancer, and at those times, we held ours close in fear that it could happen to us. We celebrated with all of the families that completed their treatment but then cried and prayed with those who relapsed. I have always felt that sharing my story would be a fear for cancer families to hear. No one wants to hear that it is a possibility that your child may die. We always want to hear survival stories. There are families just like ours who need to hear our story. The story doesn't always turn out to be a happy ending. We hurt, and there is nothing we can do about it but take our hurts to God.

I am not upset at families with cancer-free kids. I wouldn't wish cancer on anyone. There was some kind of comfort to Kahlie to be around her friends with cancer at the hospital. Everyone had the same issues like losing their hair and being swollen from prednisone. She didn't feel strange like she did when she was out in public and everyone stared at her. They weren't being mean; they were just curious about what was wrong with her.

Blessed are the merciful for they shall obtain mercy. We had so many people reach out to us with compassion and mercy in our hard times. Kahlie had great support from friends. When Kahlie lost her hair the first time, she was very insecure and embarrassed. She wore lots of hats. One of her best friends wore a hat every time that she was around her. Her friends loved her and never made fun of the way she looked; they just wanted her to be okay. We may never know what people are really going through by just looking at someone. It's just human nature to stare at someone in a wheelchair or at someone who has cancer and doesn't have any hair. Someone could have gotten the worst news of his or her life and just need a shoulder to cry on. This should be all of our prayers: "I Need Your Mercy."

CHAPTER 9

When God Took Her Home

In the final days, we stopped videoing because she was too weak and sick. That was not the way we wanted to remember her. We took a few pictures just for me to journal everything. I knew that one day I would share her story. Everyone wanted to remember her smile, quick wit, and vibrant personality. Kahlie's last Christmas season she spent the night with her cousin. Kahlie's aunt and uncle had some costumes she tried on to be silly. She put on angel wings and a halo. Her uncle took her picture. That is the picture of her everyone loves. Her uncle made many copies and has given them out to hundreds of people. It is the front cover picture of this book. What a million-dollar smile.

The last evening, Kahlie had a difficult time breathing. Her faced was glued to the oxygen tank mask. She was so weak she could hardly hold her head up. The whole family was at our house. Kahlie was in the living room and told us that she knew she was going to die. She said that she could feel her body shutting down. She said, "I'm going to die, but it's going to be okay." What a bold statement coming from a thirteen-year-old. She hoped she was in God's hands and if he wanted to bring her home, she accepted God's will. Everyone was crying, and we all felt helpless. She asked if we could take her to the hospital, so I called her doctor. As I packed for the final trip to the hospital, I just went through the motions. We got her into the van. I sat in the rear seat with her and held her hand the whole way. Somehow I also felt like I was dying that night.

When we arrived at the hospital that night, all the nurses came to see us. The look of sadness was on their faces because they knew this was the end for Kahlie on this earth. They had watched Kahlie come through so much in the past six years it was disheartening to see what was happening. My family spent the night in a vacant room next to us. I was desperate, and I wrestled with God all night while lying in bed with Kahlie. She grunted all night. I couldn't rest because I was listening to the heart monitor beep. I was in deep turmoil over God's will and my will. I begged God not to take her. I remembered when we dedicated Kahlie to the Lord in a sweet church service when she was only a few days old. We got her all dressed up in a beautiful lavender and white dress. We were all dressed up, too, and had great anticipation for her life. We had cameras all around and spirit-filled music. We were so excited to give her to God. But we really didn't know what we were doing that day because today was the real day that we had to dedicate Kahlie back to God. It wasn't pretty at all. We weren't dressed up. I had cried all of my makeup off, and there was no music. I began to pray the Lord's Prayer: "Thy kingdom come thy will be done in earth as it is in heaven." I have never prayed in full surrender as I did that morning.

Almost at the break of dawn, I came to the realization that God was going to have his way even if I prayed all night or said no all night. The monitor began to change, and I knew the time was near. The nurses went to bring my family into the room. Kason was asleep in the room with us; he wasn't aware of what was going on. We all were crying and stayed silent while listening to the heart rate monitor as it slowed down. Kahlie was uncomfortable, so I adjusted her in her bed. She seemed to want to tell me something. I asked her where she wanted to go. She pointed up. I knew in my spirit exactly what she was telling me. She told us that she loved us and then pointed up again as if she was seeing something. I told her to go rest in Jesus, and she nodded. She was in my arms in that hospital bed, and I watched her take her last breath. I was there when she entered the world and took her first breath, and I was there when she took her last.

A calm presence and peace entered the room, but it felt so final. Kahlie had overcome. She had finished her course. I had thought that they would have to put me into a straitjacket while kicking and screaming when she died, but a calm presence came over me. I was shocked and in disbelief that this was really happening. I was so disappointed and crushed. My heart was broken. God's presence was truly in the room with us that morning. The doctor came into the room to pronounce her dead, and I wanted to bathe her and wash her hair while travailing on the inside. Randy and I had our time alone with her before they took her away to the funeral home. I didn't say good-bye. I told her that I would see her later. That was the only hope I had.

Randy went into the hallway first and collapsed on the floor. I was still in the room with Kahlie. He was having a hard time. He told God that he could never preach again and that he could never preach about faith. We went to many churches, preaching that God was going to heal Kahlie. We had big faith and high hopes that if we just believed enough that God would do it. Randy was broken on the floor, and the Lord began to talk to him. He reminded Randy of a song that he used to sing when he was a teenager: "What Ever It Takes to Draw Closer to You Lord" by Lanny Wolfe. He told him that he used to sing it with such passion. The verse says, "Take the dearest things to me, if that's how it must be to draw me closer to thee. Let the disappointments come, lonely days without the sun If through sorrow more like you I'll become." The Lord told Randy that this was the time he would really have to live those words.

God wanted to reveal himself to us more than ever before. It was going to be a side of him that we'd never known. The Lord told him that "Everyone has a measure of faith to receive their miracle, something tangible that they can see as a result of prayer, but I am going to teach you a faith that when you don't get what you pray for, you will still have faith in me even though I didn't answer your prayer. You will know that I am still God, and I am in control".

We were in absolute shock about what had just happened. It didn't seem real. I have never felt so lost in my life as I did at that moment. As I walked out of the hospital room, I hugged my mom and collapsed on the floor. They put me in a wheelchair and took me down to my van. They asked us if we wanted to take Kahlie's wheelchair with us, and I said no. I wasn't in the frame of mind to make a decision, so we left it there. Her doctor told us that he was sorry and would keep in touch with us.

On our drive home, Kason woke up, and we didn't speak a word the whole ride home. I was battling in my mind and thinking, *As soon as I get home I am going to tell God how wrong he has done me.* When we arrived home, all of Kahlie's hospital equipment was in the house, and we wanted it gone that day. I ran straight to my bedroom and slammed the door. I fell prostrate on the floor. I tried to shout at God. I was so mad and angry at the fact that she had to die. How could this be his perfect plan? My intentions were to shake my fist at God. "Why? Why?" is what I wanted to say, but his spirit took over, and he began to intercede through me. I had no control at all. He prayed for me in a heavenly language. He was truly being my comforter. I felt pure agony and release at the same time. I was dying to my will at that very moment.

I wish I could say that when I got off of the floor, I felt my spirit uplifted, but he was carrying me, and the load was not going to crush or overtake me. The truth was that I felt my weakness like I had never felt before. His strength was being made perfect in my weakness. This was something that a mother and father would not get over in just one touch. Just like in Kahlie's song, we were going to need his mercy and grace to get through this.

When I was a little girl, my granny's brother died, and when they told her, she began to cry and speak in tongues. I knew that she did that when she prayed and while she was in church. We weren't in church, and she wasn't praising God. I didn't understand that as a child. As I became older, I found out that the Holy Ghost is our comforter, and he lives inside of us. He strengthens us when we are weak. I would have never made it without him. That exact thing happened to me that day. We dreaded having to tell Kason. Through the years, he was used to seeing us cry because of his sissy being sick. He wasn't sure what was going on because we had to wake him up at the hospital to go home. We told him that Kahlie had died, and she was with Jesus. We had to tell him that she was not coming back home with us. He was shocked and filled with grief. That was the most hurtful news to tell a six-year-old. We tried to console him but felt like no one could console us.

The house filled fast with family and friends to help with cleaning my house and funeral arrangements. The planning of the funeral was sudden. It was Friday morning, and we wanted to have the funeral on a Sunday, so more people could be there. I was in a fog and could not make decisions on my own. That's why we had family and friends to help us. The only thing I knew that I wanted was to have someone sing and play Kahlie's songs to honor her. As the day became night, it was all sinking in, and I felt like I wanted to die. My brother was so concerned and hurt that he stayed the night to keep an eye on us. We didn't do much sleeping that night even though I hadn't slept much in the last few days. I remember waking up and hoping and praying that it was all some bad dream, but it was real.

Visitation day was so draining for me. All of the crying and lack of sleep were catching up with me. Hundreds of people came to support and show their love for us. I didn't want to face the day of the funeral, but I had no other choice. The church was so full it was standing room only. Everyone came to celebrate our awesome girl who had blessed so many lives with her testimony, singing her songs, playing the piano and her trumpet, and writing poems. It was a beautiful service. As we drove to the graveside service, we had to pass the fire department. They were a big support to us when Randy had to be off work. His fellow workers stood by the road with the fire truck lights on and the flag half-staff. It was nice of them to honor Randy and our family and show their respect.

Knowing that my daughter—whom I hugged, touched, and kissed—was in a casket going into the ground was way too much for me to bear. The only thing I wanted to do when it was all over was to go to sleep and try to get away from the pain. Many people were still at the house, and Randy and I were in our room, grieving and sleeping.

I told Randy that I wanted to get out of town. I asked Kason where he would like to go, and he said that he wanted to go to Nickelodeon Studios and get slimed. I told him that he may not get slimed, but we could take him. That was the last place on earth I wanted to go after I buried my daughter. I just wanted to lock myself in the hotel room and cry all week. But I knew that Kason was in a lot of pain, too, and he didn't really understand everything that was going on. We wanted to do something special for him. My mom and dad went with us to Nickelodeon Studios in Florida. We walked into the show, and Kason sat with hundreds of kids on the stage to be selected to be slimed. Kason was a very little six-year-old, and a lot of kids were jumping up, screaming for them to be picked. Kason just politely raised his hand, and the host of the show picked Kason out of all of those kids. We have it all on video. We just cried because we knew that God was doing something very special for Kason and our family through our pain. I was glad the Lord gave Kason the desire of his heart that day.

When we went back to the hotel, Randy and my dad took Kason to the pool. They were just trying to keep his mind off of the loss of his sissy. I stayed in the room with my mom. As I looked down at the pool from my window, I saw a little boy who had drowned. People were doing CPR on him. I couldn't tell who it was, and I began to panic, thinking it could be Kason. Then I saw them getting out of the pool. I was so glad it wasn't Kason. My emotions were all over the place. They revived the boy, and I began to scream and cry. I fell on the floor and had a meltdown. Don't get me wrong; I didn't want that boy to die, but I was questioning God about why he chose for that little boy to live and my girl to die. It was so painful. My momma was with me, and she prayed for God to help me. She was hurting for me and for the loss of her granddaughter. Momma explained to Randy what I saw through the window, and they understood my meltdown. We held each other and cried. There were going to be many more meltdowns to come on this long and winding road of grief.

Leaving Florida and going home was going to be a long ride back. The house was so empty. It was filled with the flowers from the funeral, a big reminder of what they stood for. Even though we got away for a while, we couldn't escape the pain and the reality that Kahlie was never coming back to us. June 6, 2003, the day God took her home, forever changed our lives.

CHAPTER 10

Grieving

After Kahlie died, our whole lives changed. We were not able to function like normal human beings. Just getting out of the bed was a big thing for us. Paying bills or making a grocery list was too much for me to even think about. I was thankful that Randy was able to be off work and with us the past four months to spend our final days with our girl. We turned over our checkbook to my mom to pay our bills, and my brother went to the grocery store for us and cooked some. It was the little things that helped us out a lot.

A part of me died that I can never get back. We were a great puzzle, and she took her pieces with her. How was I supposed to put the pieces back together again? The last six years we lived a fast-pace life with a lot of doctors' appointments, hospital visits, physical therapy, occupational therapy, and church. I felt as though I had hit a concrete wall. It all came to a screeching halt. With nothing to do and nowhere to go, I felt lost. Taking care of

Kahlie had consumed my life. I had a son I loved very much to pour my life into. I didn't want to make him suffer just because I was grieving.

A couple of weeks after the funeral, the fire department asked Randy when he could come back to work. We panicked. Randy said that he wasn't ready, and I wasn't ready for him to leave us.

I told you earlier that we are not the normal kind of people. We decided for him to quit his job, and we would see where God would lead us through our grief. We had just sold our old house at a profit, and Randy knew that he could go back to the fire department at any time. He still had his lawn business. I know that sounds crazy, but we were going to need time to grieve. We didn't care. The whole world could have blown up in smoke, and it would have been okay with us because we would have been out of our misery. I know people thought we were out of our minds, but if you've never lost a child, you would never know the devastation it brings.

Each week we had friends come and pray for us to keep us strengthened in the Lord. We went to some friends' house one evening to pray, and the kids wanted to play next door at their grandpa's house. We were a little leery about letting Kason go because of our recent loss. We let him go play while we prayed. We heard a gunshot coming from where Kason was and someone hollering help. Randy was frozen. My motherly instincts were to get to my boy as fast as I could. All I could think of was, *Someone just shot my boy in the house next door.* My heart raced. I couldn't lose another child. When I got to the house next door, Kason was crying, and a little girl was crying with blood on her face. I was so worried. The grandpa tried to tell us that they were playing karate, and Kason accidently kicked the little girl in the nose. Sigh. Oh what a big relief. I grabbed him and held him close. Randy was so mad at why the man would shoot his gun to get our attention. They told us that their grandpa didn't have a phone, and that was how he got their attention in the country. We could hardly say good-bye we were so shook up. The boy almost drowning at the pool and hearing gunshots from the house where my son was were way too much for us.

For ten months we trusted God to meet our needs without Randy working at the fire department. Money was running out, and Randy went to get his job back. They told him his thirteen years of seniority would be gone, and he'd have to start over and go back to school like a rookie. We prayed about it and felt God was shutting the door for him not to go back.

We decided to sell the house even though we'd only lived there a short time. The people who sold us the house wanted to buy it back from us at asking price. Wow! We thought it was God's will for sure. At the last minute, they backed out. We had a few make offers, but they always fell through. After it had been on the market a few months, my momma and daddy called me and wanted to take us to lunch. We met with them, and she told me that she had a dream that we were not to sell our house. God would meet our needs. That day we called the Realtor and took the sign down. That month we received checks in the mail to help us pay our bills for three months. God did provide like he promised.

Randy got a job at the sheriffs' office because we had to have a full-time income coming in. I was glad that he was able to spend time with us for ten months. I knew it would be hard on him to start a new career and be back in the workforce after losing Kahlie. I spent my days trying to homeschool Kason and just make it through each day. I knew that God has something special for Kason to endure such a loss. When Kahlie was in the hospital, a minister we'd never met came to see her. He'd heard about Kahlie and wanted to pray for her. We said yes, of course. While he was praying, he leaned down to Kason, who was five years old at the time, and prayed over him, too. He told Kason that God was anointing him to preach one day. His sister's story would be a big part of his ministry, and God would get the glory.

We often talk about Kahlie. It keeps her alive in our hearts. Many people don't know what to say to parents who have lost children. Just ask us about Kahlie, and we won't be able to stop talking. It brings some kind of comfort just to talk about her. You don't even have to say a word; just be there. No one gave us a handbook on how to handle losing a child. Everyone has different experiences and deals with grief in different ways. But I will tell you that shock is always the first stage of grief. We were numbed with disbelief. Shock provides emotional protection from being overwhelmed all at once. This may last a few weeks. As the shock wears off, it's replaced with the suffering of unbelievable pain. Although excruciating and almost unbearable, it is important that you experience the pain fully and not hide it. This is the time when those who are hurting are in danger. I ran to God for my comfort and not to anything else to mask the pain.

Depression, reflection, and loneliness kick in when your family and friends are getting back to their lives. A long period of sad reflection will likely take over. This is a normal stage of grief. Don't allow anyone to tell you how long it takes to grieve. Encouragement from others does not help you during this stage of grief. There were days that I didn't get out of bed and then there were days that I pushed myself to take my son to the park or shopping. Every day was different. During that time, I realized the true magnitude of my loss, and it depressed me to the core. I found myself not wanting to talk on the phone, and I wanted to isolate myself from people. I felt like when people saw me, all they could say was, "Bless her heart, her daughter died, and she must be so sad." People didn't know how to act around me; it felt awkward.

When I reflected on the things that Kahlie did and we did together and focused on memories of the past, I felt emptiness and loneliness. One night I couldn't sleep and laid on her bed at 3:00 in the morning. I was in deep grief. I saw a vision of an eagle flying straight toward my face. It was so real that I pressed my head back into the pillow. I was wide awake seeing this. I've never had anything like that happen to me before. It must have done something to me, because I slept all night for the first time since Kahlie died. I woke up the next morning, and the Lord reminded me what he had shown me in the vision. He spoke to me with his Word. "But they that wait upon the Lord shall renew their strength: they shall mount up with wings as eagles: they shall run, and not be weary: and they shall walk, and not faint" Isaiah 40:31. I woke up a changed person. I was coming to a different stage of grief, what I call the upward turn. I started adjusting my life, knowing that Kahlie was in my future and in my past. My depression started lifting somewhat, and I felt as though I could smile about something again. I'd thought that I would never have anything to laugh about ever again. I received a phone call that same day. I was asked to speak at a women's conference. If they had called me the day before, I would have said no. But God renewed my strength.

No matter how one loses a child, whether by a prolonged illness or a sudden death, it is perhaps the most profound, the most overwhelming, and the most inconsolable of losses to deal with. It violates the natural order of things; your children are not supposed to die before you. Your love for your child is unconditional and pure. It's perhaps the most profound attachment you will ever have. If you lose a spouse, you are a widow or a widower. If you lose your parents, you are an orphan. There are no words to describe parents who have lost their children. It evokes rage at the injustice of it all. It's not fair for an innocent child to lose his or her potential and fail to see dreams fulfilled. That is why we have to trust in the Lord with all of our hearts and can't lean on our own understanding. I look back now on that time of grief and know that God was there, sustaining me.

The Bible says that "He doesn't give us the spirit of fear, but of power, love, and of a sound mind or a disciplined mind" Second Timothy 1:7. The pain was so great I could have turned to drugs and alcohol, but I never wanted to be separated from God and Kahlie for all eternity. That was the hope that never left me. Paul said that "Nothing shall separate me from the love of Christ. Shall tribulation, or distress, or persecution, or famine, or nakedness, or peril, or sword?"Romans 8:35. Paul had a true hope that he wasn't going to allow hard times to cause him to turn away from God. I am thankful for his keeping power in my life and when I wanted to make an idol out of my pain. He kept me when I could have let go.

The reconstruction and working through stage comes without you being aware of it. I became more functional, and my mind was able to think practically again. I tried to begin my life without Kahlie on a daily basis. I lived in the reality that she was never coming back to me on this earth again. I had a couple of dreams after she died. Kahlie came to our door, rang the doorbell, and knocked. I went to the door, and she was there. I kissed her and hugged her tightly. I tried to tell her that she had died, and we had a funeral for her. She gave me the biggest smile and said, "Momma, I'm not dead. I'm alive." I'm thankful for the peace it gave me to know for sure that she was alive. During this last stage of grief—of acceptance and hope—you learn to accept and deal with the reality of your situation. Acceptance does not necessarily mean instant happiness. Given the pain and the turmoil we experienced, we knew that we would never be the same ever again. I couldn't return to my carefree, untroubled self that existed before our loss. I took the Word of God and stood on his promises.

The Lord told me to get Kahlie's wheelchair back from the hospital. He told me he was going to use it for ministry. Crying, I called my mom and told her that I wanted her wheelchair back and couldn't go get it. I wasn't ready to go back. Momma went to the hospital, and when she arrived, everyone said, "Hey, Nana."

My momma asked if they still had Kahlie's wheelchair. They took her to a storage room and told her that they couldn't get rid of it. They had a feeling that we would want it back. It had her name, Kahlie Blair, embroidered on the back of the seat. We were relieved that we got it back. It had been a while, since we left it at the hospital the day she died.

Randy and I were asked to minister at my cousin's church, where he is the pastor. I did a drama with Kahlie's wheelchair. It was so emotional for me, but I was empowered by the Lord to do it. As the song begins, I'm sitting in a wheelchair as a mangled person while listening to the song "I Can Only Imagine" by Mercy Me. I began to wonder what heaven would be like healed and fully whole. As the song continues, I jump out of the chair and dance, worship, and fall to my knees to God. Toward the end of the song, I sit back into the wheelchair as if it was all a fantasy. Reality comes back, and I'm still mangled and bound to that wheelchair. I shared my story of how Kahlie is no longer in need of this wheelchair. She is present with the Lord, worshipping and dancing at the feet of Jesus. We are the ones now that can only imagine.

One day I was walking and pouring my soul out to God. He told me, "Weeping may endure for the night, but joy comes in the morning." He revealed it to me in a different way that day. He also told me that "Joy comes in the mourning." Jesus always comes to us when we are in mourning. The Bible says in Psalm 51:17, "My sacrifice, O God, is a broken spirit; a broken and contrite heart you, God, will not despise." A few months after Kahlie died, we were asked to speak at many churches. I felt like

I didn't have anything positive to say because we were broken. God had us ministering through our pain. He healed us while we ministered to others.

Since I was a teenager, I have written more than a hundred songs. I love music, and the Lord uses music to calm my soul. When Kahlie was first sick, the Lord began to rain many songs into my spirit. It was my therapy and my strength. After she died, I told God that I could never sing again. I didn't want to sing without her. I didn't feel as though I had a song in my heart anymore. The Lord said that he would give me a song in the night. That is what he did for me. He is the lifter of my head.

Two years after Kahlie's death, Randy said that the Lord told him we needed to start a church. We were helping another church at the time with some special friends. When he told me, I thought that he had lost his mind. It's easy to do something when everything lines up, but it seemed crazy to tackle pastoring a church two years after your daughter dies. The Lord gave Kahlie the name of our ministry when we were traveling to other churches. Renewing Your Hope Ministries was birthed out of a lot of pain, not knowing if she was going to live or die. We needed to keep going, as hard as it was. She was a vital part of our ministry, so how was it going to work without her? It was easy to minister when we thought things were going well for us, but when it seemed we had lost it all, it had to be by renewing our minds to keep us going. It wasn't easy, though. Like Jacob, we walk with a limp. We lean on his rod and staff every day. Renewing Your Hope Ministries helped us through these stages of grief.

Chapter 11

Ladybugs

I'm not superstitious, but I do believe that God will use whatever is close to your heart to speak to you. Ours are ladybugs. Kahlie always loved them. Since her nana called her Kahliebug when she was a toddler, it only made since to collect things with ladybugs on them. After Kahlie passed away, ladybugs began showing up in unexpected places. I was asked to attend a women's conference in Kentucky about six months after she passed away. I didn't want to go or leave my family, but I was talked into going by some close friends. When we got there, I had several ladybugs in my room. No one else had any in their rooms. I had a peace come over me that God was with me, and he was going to help me through this.

When Randy agreed to preach for the first time after her death, we were nervous about an emotional breakdown because we hadn't been to that church since Kahlie was with us. When he got up to preach, he looked up at the light fixture, and there was a ladybug, crawling around. Randy believed it was God, telling him that he was with him, and everything was going to be okay.

We went on a cross-country vacation trip. We flew to Seattle, Washington, and then drove back to Georgia. We had to stop in California because the vehicle we were in needed some minor repairs. We didn't know our way around town, so we stopped to ask where the nearest repair shop was. As I rolled down my window, a ladybug flew in and landed on my leg. I knew at that moment that no matter where we were, God was taking care of us.

My mom went back to college in her fifties, and when she graduated, the whole family went to the ceremony. As I went to sit down, a ladybug was in my seat. I was sad that Kahlie wasn't there to celebrate with us, but God has always used ladybugs to say, "I am here, and it's going to be okay." Many times out of nowhere, ladybugs land on my clothes or on my hand. It seems that no matter where I am, I have an encounter with them. I know these stories may seem far-fetched, but they are real. Many times through the years ladybugs are present. God will always speak to us however he wants. We just need to be waiting and listening.

I feel like every time a ladybug shows up it's a sign between God, Kahlie, and our family. It's a reminder to me and a God whisper to be still and know that he is God. They always show up on special events, holidays, or just when I need a special word of confirmation. When I was young, my daddy had a CB radio. My name, or handle as they call it, was Little Ladybug. That was the beginning and the introduction of our lives with ladybugs.

On Kahlie's last Christmas, she wanted a silver trumpet. She loved playing so much. She was so excited when she opened it up. It was her dream trumpet, the one she always wanted. By that time, she had been playing for five years. That was a great Christmas for our family. We didn't know that in fewer than six months, Kahlie's silver trumpet would be played by a friend at her funeral. I still have it in the case in her closet. Maybe one day it will be used for God's glory again.

Kahlie loved to help me cook and set the table. Family meals were her favorite times. It was always nice when she wasn't in the hospital, and we were all home together. We all have a great memory that we hold onto when we lose someone we love very much. Kahlie and I were very close. She was also close to her daddy and brother. I loved watching them together. They sang "Butterfly Kisses." They played silly games that only we would understand. Her daddy took her on father and daughter dates. The last date they went on was to Outback Steak House. She had a love for steak, just like her daddy. When she was well, she had a good appetite. Toward the end of her life, we were in bed together, and she grabbed a piece of paper and started writing down her favorite foods that she wanted us to cook when she started feeling better. It broke my heart, but we laughed and laughed as if we were eating all of that food right then. I still have that list of food.

I had a book called *Daily Medicine.* It was Scriptures that I would read to her throughout the day, in the morning, afternoon, and at night. She always asked me to read it to her. It gave her comfort. Before Kahlie relapsed for the last time, we were going to record all of her songs and a few of mine at a studio. We had it all set up. As she became sicker, her voice became weaker. We have her practicing on video, and we hold onto it dearly.

My sister-in-law wanted me to go with her to a women's retreat about four years after Kahlie died. I went to receive something from the Lord. Even though I loved God and worked in ministry as a pastor's wife, I secretly felt that I hated my life without Kahlie in it. I lived every day still wishing my life could have been different. It was hindering my harvest, but I felt like that was the way it was always going to be. I sat in the middle of the crowd at one of the services, and the woman who was speaking called me to the front. She told me that God was giving me a good life and to receive what God had for me. She didn't know that my words under my breath every day were, "I hate my life! I hate my life!" As she prayed for me, she said, "It's a good life! It's a good life!" I knew that God was repeating it twice for me to reverse what I had been telling myself. That day I knew that even when the most devastating thing happens in your life, having God in it makes it better. I just needed to change the way I was thinking every day. It didn't mean that I wasn't going to think about her anymore. I just had to see through God's eyes that despite my loss, God still had great things in store for me and my family.

I had a fear of going back to the hospital after Kahlie died. I'm a pastor's wife. How am I going to go visit the sick? A few years later, Randy's granny wasn't doing well. She was in the hospital for a week, and it didn't look like she was going to make it. I battled and felt guilty for not going up there to see her. I broke down one day and went. I got one of Randy's cousins to meet us there. As I went, I felt empowered by God. Randy's cousin and I sang "Amazing Grace" to her, and though unconscious, she had tears rolling down her face. She passed away the next day. I know that she was waiting on me to come see her before she left this world.

Randy's other grandmother, whom we all called Maw, was almost ninety-seven years old and lived a good, healthy life, but she was starting to slow down a lot. When it came time for her to pass away, we all gathered around her bed. I was happy for her to be able to go see the Lord. Her husband and two children had gone before her. She was the second human being I saw take their last breath right in front of me. I remember her telling me about her experience with losing two adult children. It grieved her heart. I saw her cry and talk about them often. One of her children who died was my husband's mother. I never met her because she passed away two years before Randy and I met. I feel like God put that special lady in my life to help me because he knew that I was going to lose a child also. The Lord brought her through, and I knew that he would do the same for me. I lost my granny when I was seventeen years old, and I missed her a lot. It left a big void in our family. Maw came in and became the grandmother I didn't have anymore.

Randy's mother died when he was seventeen years old. He had to deal with being a young man without a parent. When Kahlie died, Randy was in his own turmoil, wrestling with God on why he had to take his momma and his daughter. He felt it wasn't fair. Deuteronomy 32:4 reads, "He is the rock, his work is perfect: for all his ways are judgment: a God of truth and without iniquity, just and right is he." God is a just God. God is more interested in changing our characters than changing our circumstances. Everything God does is for his glory. He never makes mistakes!

When I was eighteen years old, I was invited to go visit a church with some friends. When I walked in, Randy was there. The Lord told Randy that I was going to be his wife. He laughed because he thought it was just him thinking it to himself. He had never seen me before. I changed churches and started attending every service. I was there for almost a year, seeking God and not looking for a relationship. Randy was a young man in the church that I thought was twelve years old; he was very young looking. I couldn't believe it when I found out that he was nineteen. He was eight months older than I. His sister tried to get me to go out to eat with them after church. I always declined unless we all went out as a large crowd. I had been there a year by then, and at one service, Randy was getting a great blessing. I watched him be free in the spirit to cry, dance, and praise God. While he was getting blessed, he told God that he thought he told him that I was going to be his wife. I hadn't even spoken much to him. The song that was being sung in the service was about seeking first the kingdom of God and his righteousness, and all things will be added unto you. Randy cried out to God to keep him first in his life. After the service was over, I didn't even know what God and Randy had been talking about, but I felt to give Randy my phone number. I watched as he was a teenager, just like me, wanting to serve God, and that meant a lot to me. We only dated four months before we were married on June 1, 1989. I guess God telling Randy I was going to be his wife was very true.

After we married, we compared stories about where we had lived and friends we had growing up. We knew a lot of the same people, but our paths had never crossed. I used to go to a youth prayer service every week that was right across the street from where he lived. His uncle came to my church when I was little, and Randy came to visit with him many times. We were the same age, so we would have been in the same Sunday school class. I was at a friend's house one day when I was in junior high school and her brother and a friend he called Bubba came into the house. I never came out of my friend's room to see who it was. My friend's brother and Bubba knew that a girl named Tonia was in the house. Later, I found out that my husband was Bubba. Randy is the baby brother of two sisters, so that is why they call him— Bubba. We were meant to be together. I am thankful God chose him to be a witness with me and share all of my life's experiences, good and bad.

CHAPTER 12

What I've Learned Along the Way

I've wanted to write this book but have fought doing so for years. I felt that I had a voice and story to tell, but I also knew that it was going to be very painful to relive each moment. We all wanted that happy ending to the story, especially church people. I wished that our story was different and Kahlie was healed and could walk, sing, play her instruments and tell the whole world about God's goodness. We didn't get that kind of ending. It wasn't because of our lack of faith or anything that we did. We fasted until we lost weight. We cried until we couldn't cry anymore. We prayed until our knees hurt, and our legs fell asleep. I'm not saying not to pray and believe until the end. I'm just saying that in the end, pray God's will be done. It was God's will, and he worked something good out of it. I'll never know the real reason God took

Kahlie from us, but I sure have a hope that I will spend eternity worshipping God with her. That is my happy ending!

I want to live to see the work of God finished in my life. The one thing I knew was that I would write this book and tell my story in memory of my precious daughter. I have been through many hard times in life, and you may have too. I have had a hard time fighting that "Woe is me" attitude. I have to keep reminding myself that God is for me, and if he is for me, who can be against me?

When I was a little girl, I knew God had something special for me to do. I was sensitive to his spirit and had a genuine love for him. I was told as a young girl that I would have the gift of healing. That seemed strange to me given the fact that I couldn't pray the healing into my daughter. But now I have learned that God has used me to speak his word to others, and that is how people's hearts and souls are healed. I want to be an encourager to others and let them know that no matter what they're going through, God can renew their hope every day. I thought that Kahlie would have impacted the world if she had lived longer. Many have told us that she accomplished more in thirteen years than a person who has lived ninety years.

I'm not an expert, and I don't have a psychology degree. I am a real mother who has gone through the real pain of losing her child. There is not one way to handle it. There is no cookie-cutter plan. The one thing I have learned along the way is that in this life, we will have tribulations. But Jesus said, "Be of good cheer I have overcome the world" John 16:33 .We as Christians always want the easy way out. Let's just pray the problem away as fast as we can. No pain and no heartache. God uses these trials in our lives to make us more like him. First Peter 5:10 reminds us that "After that you have suffered awhile, make you perfect, establish, and settle you."

I have learned that fighting the cross you have to carry will only bring turmoil. I no longer want to fight the cross. I choose to cling to the cross because it is the power of God. Jesus said to deny yourself and take up your cross and follow me. Crosses come in different ways. You may have lost a child. You may have buried your spouse. You may have a medical problem. You may have gotten a divorce, or you may have lost your job. No matter what the cross is, we have to have a good attitude toward it. It is not there to kill you; It's there to save you. Second Corinthians 1:6 tells us, "whether we be afflicted, it is for your consolation and salvation which is effectual in the enduring of the same sufferings which we also suffer: or whether we be comforted, it is for your consolation and salvation." When Jesus was on the cross, there were two men beside him. One wanted to come off the cross because he felt that he didn't deserve death. He told Jesus that if he is the son of God to save him and himself. One had a good attitude towards the cross as if he knew that he deserved death. He asked if he would remember him when he went into his kingdom. Jesus told him that he would be with him in paradise. I don't get to pick my cross. It is handed to me to carry. I pray the Lord helps me have a good attitude toward my cross at all times. At first I felt I didn't deserve to be the one who lost a child. I wanted to come down from my cross. Jesus has been changing my spirit on the cross, and now I know that I do deserve death, but Jesus gives me life and a reward in exchange for all my suffering.

Four years after Kahlie died, I had a job presented to me by someone at the police department at Mercer University. I had been a stay-at-home mom for seventeen years, and I homeschooled my children. I catered some on the side and answered calls for Randy's Lawn Service, so I was already busy. We also pastor a church. Kason was eleven at the time, so I said that I would pray about it. That was on a Friday. Monday morning, they called and asked me where my online application was. I told them that I hadn't submitted it. I felt a push in my spirit to go ahead and do it, but I wanted to know for sure that it was God. The next day they called me for an interview. I went to the interview, and the woman at the front desk looked at me as though she had seen a ghost. She told me that she had a dream, and I was the one they hired for the position. I wanted to cry, but I didn't want to mess up my makeup. The interview went great. I wasn't home but a few moments before I received the call saying that I was hired. They asked me if I could start Monday and I said yes I could. That was a God thing. Kason and I had separation anxiety at first because I had never been away from him before, but in the end, it was good for both of us.

Randy was at the sheriff's office and ready for a change. He told me that he wanted to put in his resignation, but he didn't have anywhere else to go. Randy is a lot like Peter in the Bible. He's not afraid to jump ship if he feels like the Lord is asking him to. I wasn't happy with his great faith. We even had words about it. He missed some church services because of work, and it was hindering him from being the pastor he wanted to be.

During one service, I was worshipping through singing. Every time we got to the part of the song that said, "I'm surrendering my all, I surrender to the King," I felt as though I hadn't surrendered Randy, saying that God told him to leave his job. I came off the keyboard that morning and began to worship God. He spoke these words to me: "Don't kick against the pricks with Randy. I told him to leave his job. Trust in me; I will provide." I had such a release and was blessed beyond measure. After I composed myself, I went straight to Randy and told him what the Lord spoke to me. We cried and had such peace knowing that we were being directed by God.

The next week, Randy turned in his resignation in at the sheriff's office. After he was done, he dropped by to see me at work. My chief got word that he was leaving his job and offered him a part-time position. A position had temporarily opened up because someone was called to the military for a while. Randy started working at the police department part time and then someone retired, and a full-time position opened up. It wasn't long before Randy was promoted to sergeant. I know that God was in control of our lives. Randy got a position where he wouldn't miss church anymore. Our steps are ordered from God. He sees all and knows all.

As I write these words, I feel the spirit of God moving on me to encourage everyone to keep fighting the good fight of faith. The reason it's a good fight is because it's a fixed fight. We have already won. We just have to keep pressing to stay in the fight.

Stay faithful no matter what takes place in your life because you will get the worst news of your life. You will have a trial that will knock you down. You will sometimes doubt God's plan. If you haven't, then you've never been through much of anything.

God reveals what's in our hearts in the hard times of life. God only allows them and exposes our hearts to bring us closer to him. I have learned not to stay in the why because it only keeps you in confusion. We just have to trust that God knows best. I have learned to cherish each and every moment with my family. My children are gifts from God, and I am so proud of the gifts that are working in my son and that worked in Kahlie. Loving my children came very easily for me. If all I was called to do in this life was to be Kahlie and Kason's mom, I have fulfilled God's purpose. They are my world.

I cherish the memories that I have with my kids. All I have now are pictures and videos of Kahlie. She skated in the kitchen while I was cooking. Danced like there was no tomorrow, and sang at the top of her lungs. She literally laughed out loud. She would wear three outfits a day and use two towels while taking a shower. There was time I had to get her to clean up her messy room. We get caught up in the chaos of life and worry about doing all their laundry and yelling for your teenagers to clean their rooms. Today her room is the cleanest room in the house because she's not here to use it. I would give anything just to have her here, doing all those crazy things that she used to do. I have learned to value time because it passes so quickly.

I've learned never to tell God what you will not do. As I have said before, I told the Lord that I would never sing again without Kahlie. About two months after she died, I heard a song in my head that I had never heard before. I thought that God was giving me another song to write. As I began to get the lyrics to write them down, it was as if I was hearing Kahlie singing it to me from heaven. It was so powerful. The song was coming so fast I couldn't write it fast enough, and all I could do was cry.

Resting in His Arms

It's been a long journey not knowing
where the road will take me.
It wasn't easy trusting God in times of trouble.
It's not worthy to compare; it's not worthy
to compare to where I am.
I'm resting in the arms of the Lord.
No more pain, and no more sorrow.
I've fought a good fight; I've kept the faith.
I have my reward.

At first I didn't want to die,
staying with the ones who loved me,
and then I saw the Lord.
He said come to me, and I said I'll go and find my rest.

Copyright by Tonia Wilkes

That whole song was written with music, and all only took about five minutes. I knew that song came from heaven. The wound was so fresh and the pain so great that I vowed never to sing again out of my hurt and pain. God showed me that day that my life was not my own because I belonged to him, and he was going to use me in a great way for his kingdom. He was just going to use my loss to do it. At that time, I didn't feel worthy of him using me because I knew all of the pent-up rage caused when he took the most precious thing from me. That was all I could feel inside of me. What I've learned was God's mercy overlooked my frailty. He knew that it was not going to be by power or might, but it was going to be by his spirit that everything he was working in me would be accomplished.

Kahlie often wrote her feelings down in a journal. When she was twelve years old, she wrote a poem I found after she died. It's like she is writing about the day she dies, eight months exactly.

He Knows Why

Bless the day when he shall come.
I'll be shining like the sun
As I lay my head to rest.
I wonder if it's only a test.
I often wonder why
I always seem to cry.
He's the one to listen,
And he knows why.

Copyright by Kahlie Wilkes 10-10-02

It was almost like God was putting in her spirit that something was going to happen. She died right as the sun was coming up, and she did lay her head to go rest in Jesus. I'm glad that she always had a hope that he knows why.

Kahlie was a very curious young girl, but she also had great faith in God. Here are a couple more poems I want to share.

TONIA WILKES

I Wonder Why

I wonder why the sky is blue.
I guess that no one has a clue.
I wonder why it has to rain.
It's like each drop is for our pain.
Now I know it's God's creation,
Every color.
He made this nation.
Everything has a purpose,
So I don't have to wonder why.

Copyright by Kahlie Wilkes

Like Me

If you were like me,
How would this world be?
It would be dull.
It would be lame.
With no one else to give the blame,
Everyone would have the same answers.
It wouldn't be right.
We would all want to fight.
Our personalities would clash.
God made me,
So I love who I am.
No one in this world could be like me.

Copyright by Kahlie Wilkes

88

Chapter 13

Stayin' Alive

I was a seventies child, and we loved the Bee Gees. One year Kahlie bought her daddy all of their music. Our family's theme song is "Stayin' Alive." It resonates with everything we have been through. No matter how hard life gets, we have God.

Moses saw the burning bush in the desert. It never burnt up because God was in the bush. God is in us, and no matter how hot the flames are, we can't burn up. Isaiah 43:2 reads, "When thou passest through the waters, I will be with thee: and through the rivers, they shall not overflow thee: When thou walkest through the fire, thou shalt not be burned: neither shall the flames kindle upon thee." It is the fire that causes us to be refined and more like him. The fire doesn't feel good to our carnal mind. Our natural response is to run away from the fire to stay alive, but the fire is what it takes for us to live. If we try to save our lived, we will lose it. And if we lose our lives, we will find it. God is our refiners' fire, and if we just stand in the fire, the only thing that will be burned is the chaff, or our carnal way of thinking, and all the things that have us bound. God is in control of how hot it gets. He doesn't allow it to burn us up. That is his grace.

I am blessed to say that my son, Kason, preaches the gospel; plays the drums, guitar, and piano; sings; and teaches Bible study online. I bragged because I really wanted to brag on God. Through the fire in all of our lives, God has made something beautiful out of it. The Lord said that he would give us beauty for ashes. All I have to offer him are my ashes.

When Kason was seventeen, he wrote a song called "Crazy Love." It describes how much the Lord loves us and all the ways he shows us every day. His love sometimes brings fire our way to refine us. When the fire comes, we shouldn't think it as strange thing. First Peter 4:2–3 tells us, "Beloved, think it not strange concerning the fiery trial which is to try you, as though some strange thing happened unto you: But rejoice, inasmuch as ye are partakers of Christ's sufferings; that, when his glory shall be revealed, ye may be glad also with exceeding joy."

God is our architect. An architect designs and overseas the construction of buildings. We are the building or temple God is working on. He plans, designs, and overseas our lives in every way. He knows how much pressure we can handle, and when we think it is too much to bear, in him we cannot crumble because we are built on the Rock. It will forever stand. God's grace will always be sufficient. There have been many times in my life when I thought I couldn't handle all the weight. Then I'm reminded of what the Lord said: "Come unto me, all ye that labour and are heavy laden, and I will give you rest. Take my yoke upon you, and learn of me: for I am meek and lowly in heart: and ye shall find rest unto your souls. For my yolk is easy, and my burden is light" Matthew 11:28-29. As long as we come to him, we'll have a lighter load to carry. I couldn't have imagined going through all that I have been through if the Lord had not carried me. Kahlie used to sing a song that said, "Carry me through the storm." She knew it was God who carried her through until she passed away.

She had a lively hope and knew without a doubt where she was going. A few weeks before Kahlie died, she and her nana were riding down the road, and heard a song "Just Find Jesus, That's Where I'll Be." It was a song about going to heaven and wanting to be with Jesus. Kahlie began to cry, listening to the song for the first time. She told her nana to just find Jesus, and that's where she would be. My mom pulled over for them to have that special moment of hope together.

Many people have gone through loss just as we have. Many times I've second-guessed if anyone would care about our story. Kahlie dies at the end. I've wondered what was so different about our lives, and it always goes back to hope. We have hope! We all want our miracle and are so desperate for it. Many get their miracle, but there are some like us who never get theirs, and are left with many unknown answers of why God chooses to give to some and not to others. God can and does have the power to heal, but sometimes God doesn't because he has a different plan for our lives. We have a hope in God who has a perfect plan, but sometimes his plan is unknown to us. He has plans for our lives, plans for peace and not evil, and plans to give us an expected end. Life is never perfect, but you can conquer the world as long as you have God and each other.

I felt it was only appropriate to end this book with thirteen chapters. Kahlie lived about thirteen-and-a-half years and fulfilled everything that God had called her to be. So I felt that her story was worth a powerful thirteen chapters.

I will never see Kahlie grow into the beautiful woman that I knew she would be. I missed out on her graduation, getting married, having children, seeing her in ministry, playing her instruments, and writing and singing more songs. I can't stay in the stage of what I have missed out on. I am looking for a city whose maker and builder is God, and that's where she is. That is what I look forward to the most. Kahlie and I had a saying, "I love you to the moon and back." She was so competitive that she wanted to love me more, so she would say, "a million, trillion, and gazillion times." Oh how I would love to hear her say that again. Kahlie knew that she was loved, and we did everything we could to help her.

I had the privilege of being Kahlie's momma for thirteen and-a-half years. We shared much laughter and many tears. Our children are treasures from God, and I'm glad that God has one of my treasures, and she is safe with him for all eternity. The Bible tells us not to lay up our treasure for ourselves upon the earth, but to lay up treasures in heaven. The treasure we have here on earth is not eternal, but the treasures we have with God are eternal.

I ran a 5k with some friends with cancer for kids in memory of Kahlie. As I neared the finish line, our family theme song—"Stayin' Alive"—came on. I believe God has a sense of humor. He knew how much that song meant to me and Kahlie. People were watching our lives, and some thought that we would fall apart when Kahlie died. But I have found a secret place in him, and that is my secret to "Stayin' Alive"!

About the Author

Tonia Wilkes was born in Macon, Georgia. She is a wife, mother, and the wife of the pastor of Renewing Your Hope Ministries. She plays the piano, writes songs, and is the praise and worship leader at her church. Her number-one passion is helping others find hope in Jesus. She shares her story so that others who have been through a difficult time in life can grieve and then move on toward renewing their hopes.

31996896R10071

Made in the USA
Middletown, DE
19 May 2016